PENGUIN BOOKS

LETTERS FROM AMERICA

Alistair Cooke was born in Manchester in 1908 and educated at Jesus College, Cambridge, Yale and Harvard Universities. In 1938, after completing three years with the B B C as Film Critic, he took up his present position as Special Correspondent. Other appointments include Special Correspondent on American Affairs for *The Times*, 1938–41, American feature writer for the *Daily Herald*, 1941–4, U N Correspondent for the *Manchester Guardian* (now the *Guardian*), 1945–8, and Chief Correspondent in the U S A, 1948–72. Among the many awards he has received for his work are the Peabody Award, 1952 and 1972, the Writers' Guild Award for the best documentary in 1972, the Dimbleby Award, four Emmy Awards and the Benjamin Franklin Award, all in 1973. Alistair Cooke received an Honorary K.B.E. in 1973, an Honorary LL.D. from Edinburgh and Manchester and an Honorary Litt.D. from St Andrews University in 1975.

Alistair Cooke's 'Letter from America' has been a pleasure for millions of listeners throughout the world for over thirty years. Penguin have also published two other collections of the letters, *Talk About America* and *The Americans*. In 1972 his T V series on America met with a resounding world-wide success and this was followed by an equally successful book based on the series, *Alistair Cooke's America*. Alistair Cooke settled in America in 1937 and he has lived in New York ever since.

ALISTAIR COOKE

Letters from America

1946–1951

PENGUIN BOOKS

Penguin Books Ltd, Harmondsworth, Middlesex, England
Penguin Books, 625 Madison Avenue, New York, New York 10022, U.S.A.
Penguin Books Australia Ltd, Ringwood, Victoria, Australia
Penguin Books Canada Ltd, 2801 John Street, Markham, Ontario, Canada, L3R 1B4
Penguin Books (N.Z.) Ltd, 182–190 Wairau Road, Auckland 10, New Zealand

—

First published by Rupert Hart-Davis 1951
Published in Penguin Books 1981
Reprinted 1981

—

—

Made and printed in Great Britain by
Richard Clay (The Chaucer Press) Ltd,
Bungay, Suffolk
Set in Linotype Times

CONTENTS

5

CONTENTS

TO THE BRITISH READER

Some months after the war was over the B.B.C. asked me to go to London and discuss the sort of broadcasting I might do in what was then called the peace. I had been talking about America to Britain since 1934 and from America to Britain since three years after that. My one-man band met the same fate as everybody else's in the autumn of 1939. And through the war years I doubled in brass and learned to play the solemn trombone of a political commentator. Politics will undoubtedly bedevil us all till the day we die, but when General MacArthur stood on the deck of the *Missouri* and said in his resounding baritone, 'These proceedings are closed', I took him at his word and, like most other people, yearned to get back to the important things in life. Even the prospect of early annihilation should not keep us from making the most of our days on this unhappy planet. In the best of times, our days are numbered, anyway. And it would be a crime against Nature for any generation to take the world crisis so solemnly that it puts off enjoying those things for which we were presumably designed in the first place, and which the gravest statesman and the hoarsest politicians hope to make available to all men in the end : I mean the opportunity to do good work, to fall in love, to enjoy friends, to sit under trees, to read, to hit a ball and bounce the baby.

The suspicion that these things are what most men and women everywhere want led me to suggest, in London in 1946, that Britons might be more honestly enticed into an interest in America and Americans by hearing about their way of life and their tastes in these fundamental things than by suffering instruction in the procedures of the American Senate and the subtleties of the corn-hog ratio. Mr Lindsay Wellington, then director of the Home Service, responded so promptly to this that he suggested I forget politics altogether and accept an assignment to talk about anything and everything in America that interested me. To do this for a large and very mixed audience, ranging from shrewd bishops to honest carpenters, was a challenge to explain in the simplest and most vivid terms the passions, the manners, the flavour of another nation's way of life. It was a formidable assignment, for though a man might make sense of his travels in his own way for his own friends, broadcasting demands of him, if he respects the medium at all, that, as the old Greek had it, he 'think like a wise man and talk in the language of the people'. I don't know whether this has ever been done, except at various times by minstrels, the greatest religious teachers and comedians of genius.

But out of this bold ambition grew a series of weekly talks to Britain which I called Letters from America. They were commissioned in March 1946 for a tentative run of thirteen weeks; and by the grace of the B.B.C., the receptiveness of the British listener, and the stubborn endurance of the pound sterling, they still at this writing go on. After a year or two the number of listeners asking for copies of scripts began to strain the mimeographing resources of the B.B.C.'s New York office. Some people took so kindly to them that they urged me to put them out as a book. This has the same effect on a broadcaster as a nomination for the Presidency of the United States on a first-class cement manufacturer. The thing is patently absurd except to his cronies, but the idea first flatters, then haunts him, and he ends by feeling he must accept a sacred duty to save the Republic.

Publishers began to massage me and lonely widows to cajole me until it seemed churlish to resist. There was, however, a more honest flattery that gave me pause. A good many of the letters I have had from listeners to this series were from people who can hardly put pen to paper. Their taste seemed to coincide with my own: they had got pleasure from talks which I felt had managed to convey some human experience in a language most people can understand. These successes averaged about one in five, but they are not necessarily the ones that look best in print. But by the time the series had run to two hundred there appeared to be a good handful that would survive the translation into black and white. Accordingly, the pieces that follow were selected by this test. They were chosen on no other principle, though I have tried to include pieces about the things that first puzzle the visiting European, so that the book can be taken as a painless introduction to living in the United States. I have naturally succumbed to the pieces that produced the heaviest fan mail. And though I can find no justification for including a piece of reporting that is no practical help to anybody but a kidnapper, the mail was enormous after the talk I have here called 'A Baby is Missing'.

I have given some sort of grammatical shape to sentences that ended nowhere, as sentences do in life. And where I failed to say something tricky in a simple way, I have made so bold as to use words I would never use before a microphone, but which should not stump the small sophisticated race known as book-readers. Otherwise, except for a little trimming and polishing, these pieces appear here as they were broadcast. In their original form, a few of them were printed in the *Listener*. I ought to mention that the last anecdote, about the San Diego tattooist, in the piece called 'Six Typical Americans', had to be discreetly bowdlerized for the strong, silent family which is presumed to be the backbone of the radio audience. The reader, however, is not bound to finish that essay, especially after this warning. I merely wish to note for the record that the anecdote is here set down for the first time in all its naked truth.

Most of these pieces were written at the end of a week's work without my knowing, as I faced the typewriter, what I was going to talk about. But they were all written in freedom and in pleasure. They were then taken and read aloud to the reigning captain of the B.B.C.'s New York garrison. These gentlemen tolerated my briefs in the natives' behalf with singular good nature and revolted rarely, and then only in the most gentlemanly way, against what they thought revolting. They were fine specimens of their race, and I have no doubt their occasional revulsions saved me from offending a large part of the population of the British Isles. I should like to pay my respects in particular to Norman Luker and Henry Straker, and to two able *gauleiters* (recruited respectively from New

9

Jersey and Georgia) who performed the same service: Annette Ebsen and Sam Slate.

For the rest, this book belongs to the people who sponsored it: the brave, tolerant and courteous people of Britain, who after ten years of austerity and four of being poor relations could yet choose to sit down on Friday evenings and want to understand the foibles of the rich uncle across the seas.

A.C.

Nassau Point, Long Island
Summer, 1951

GETTING AWAY FROM IT ALL

The real end of the American year is not the thirty-first of December, but the old festival of Labour Day. It is the day when the summer is put away, the swimming-trunks squeezed for the last time, the ash-trays in country cottages filled with mouse-seed and rat-paste, the storm-doors hammered into place, the lock turned for the last time on your private world of sun and sand and picnics and the pride of growing children. Labour Day brings you back to the world of schools and offices, to sniffling colds and insurance policies, to taxes and radio commentators, to dark nights and the dark horizon of politics.

We sat around for the last time in our cottage at the end of Long Island. We had brought in the furniture from off the porch and the rusty barbecue grill we haven't used in four years but always put out in the sun at the beginning of summer as a symbol of our pioneer instincts. We had phoned the electric company to turn off the current. Called the phone company to disconnect same. Left a note for the garbage-man, same for the milkman. What else has to be done? Defrost and clean the refrigerator. Draw the curtains across the windows on the east and west sides. Sprinkle moth-flakes on the rugs. Try to hide a smelly fishing-rod in a dark closet, and fail — your wife coming at you saying, 'Could this be bait?' It is. It is a poor, dried-up piece of squid that was chewed on by a whole school of porgies and sucked dry.

We sit around finishing a last bite. The baby is snoring placidly in a house reeking of camphor and good old mouse-paste. We bury and burn the last load of garbage. We pack the car while we wait for the baby to wake. Some of the grasses on the dunes have started to turn the fall colours. So children who normally treat them as considerately as bulldozers now develop a collector's passion for bayberry and pine branches and feather-grass. Somebody sees a gramophone record worn

11

so grey you'd think it had been played with a poker. It is 'Good Night, Irene', and it too is suddenly an object of tenderness. We finally leave, with the rear end of the borrowed station-wagon looking like an army camouflage squad, bushes and plants and a bedstead growing out of each side of 'Good Night, Irene'. We are on our way.

We stop and say good-bye to Mrs Horton, who sells eggs and collects antiques and whose family has farmed the same plot since 1649 – not so hot, perhaps, to a European, but impressive to us. We wish a good winter to the Ryskos, who sell groceries; to Grathwohl, the builder and sometime carpenter; to the Doroski brothers, who run a gas and service station; to Josie Wanowski, the little bent old toothless Polish woman who has taken in washing these many years and for many of them kept a crippled husband, and who raised four astonishingly handsome children, two straight beautiful girls with shining teeth, who might be movie starlets but are in fact a nurse and a schoolteacher; two boys, one in college, one ex-army air forces.

It is much the same as any other leave-taking in the fall. But there is an ominous note or two. The bank manager is off to Riverhead: there is a meeting of the new civil defence evacuation committee – a committee, that is, to plan the evacuation of doomed New Yorkers to the potato-fields of Long Island. A young man who came out of the Navy four years ago, who chose to be a potato-farmer the year of the big drought and went into debt for two thousand dollars, is not around any more. His troubles were all scattered by a letter one morning from the President of the United States, beginning – 'Greetings!' – a cordial invitation to come back into the service, or else. Eddie, the boy who drives the grocer's delivery truck, says 'Well, I'd better say good-bye', in a strange shy way. He too has had his call.

These little things give you a shock, and you wonder about them on the way up to the city. Everything looks like the familiar fall, the maples turning, a milky stream of smoke from burning leaves curling up into a blue, bottomless sky. But as the swift twilight comes on we are at the end of the parkway, past La Guardia Field, over the Triboro Bridge, and there are the vertical city and the plunging spires: New York again, splendid as ever in the autumn light. Not quite the same, though. We curve round and down off the bridge and pass a billboard advertising a new de luxe apartment-building some- where. The big sign has stars against the features it is specially proud of: thermostat heat control in each flat; all-electric kitchen, with deep freeze, laundry and dish-washing machines, and garbage-disposal unit; air-conditioned units available in summer; two bathrooms for every four rooms. The last item, the last star, says: 'Adequate sub-basement atomic bomb- shelter'. One of the children reads it aloud, and it makes a pompous sound, so that the baby claps her hands and chortles like a wise old man. And we all laugh.

Back in the city, people with copper tans who ought to be congratulating themselves on being able in the first place to get away from the New York summer, began in recent years to find themselves fingering the real-estate sections of the Sun- day papers and peering through advertisements for 'desirable country houses'. Why should lucky and comfortable people be so fretful and restless for more idleness? It was not idleness such people sought but a more dreadful thing: safety. Lately the phrase 'getting away from it all' has taken on a sadder and more furtive meaning in the minds of parents who live in industrial cities. It needs no winks or meaningful glances to arouse a fear that everybody feels and a few talk openly about. It is the padding fear of the atom bomb.

I heard of a man who lives in Washington who had quit his job, fallen back on his savings, bought a little place deep in the hills of Arkansas and gone off there to farm with his wife and five children. Far off in the Black Hills of South Dakota, some pessimist as thoughtful as Noah has bought a mountain cave and invited prudent couples – one male, one female – to abandon their regular lives and batten down underground at an annual cost of two thousand five hundred dollars per per- son, all found. This may appear to be the furthest pole of lunacy. But during the San Francisco organizing conference of the United Nations, the citizens of the Black Hills, bidding for a lasting fame as the chosen headquarters of the United

Nations, challenged the delegations with maps (Dakotas projection) to find a spot anywhere in the United States more swiftly accessible by air to Moscow, Cairo, Tokyo or London. Maybe this pessimist was acting from the same melancholy discovery.

Then in the late nineteen-forties businessmen caught the epidemic. Businessmen, I should say, who have factories in the East, in the ring of cities round the southern rim of the Great Lakes, or out on the Coast. An aircraft company in Bridgeport, Connecticut, announced it had decided to move bag and baggage to Dallas, Texas. Now, this is quite an undertaking. The company worked on a million and a half square feet. Its factory cost ten million dollars. It employed about ten thousand people. The company invited its skilled workers to go with it. As an American migration, this one would not be without its epic and humorous side. Bridgeport is a typical New England industrial city, except for the untypical fact that it has a socialist government. Its workers are mostly of Italian and Czech, Hungarian and Polish stock. They are used to cold winters and New England ways. It would be quite a sight to see them in West Texas, mimicking the Texas accent, being baffled by the Mexican foods, wondering when the hot dry winds of spring and the steaming misery of summer would ever end in – as the song says – 'that Texas town that never seen ice or snow'. For a few excitable weeks, the unskilled men had a happy time joshing their superior brothers who had signed up to go. They bandied around the nicknames Sagebrush, and Tex, and 'Hi, there, Dallas!' Jokers appeared in ten-gallon hats and called a work-gang 'you-all'. But however gay the workers felt, the company's announcement caused a nasty jolt to other defence industries along the East Coast. Any company that would make a move as dramatic and costly as that must, they figured, have 'heard something'. The Defense Department was rattled by telephone inquiries verging between anxiety and hysteria. The callers were told in as non-committal a way as possible that there was no 'immediate' plan to go underground, to move industrial cities, to decentralize the basic industries that surround the Great Lakes. It was made officially plain that the Bridgeport company had made up its own mind

14

and the National Security Resources Board had given its nod. The company's work had to do with testing jet-planes, and the directors had decided that the congested seaboard was a poor place to accommodate, without an expensive new airport, the special and alarming habits of jets. The Texas central plain is – if Texans will pardon the expression – flatter than Kansas. It seemed just right. But many industries, big and little, leaped to the conclusion which they dread and which – by the peculiar chemistry of deep fear – they half-hope to have fulfilled.

The telling point about the Bridgeport story is, I think, the current emotional disposition to believe the worst. The atomic age offers us the raw material of a civilization larger, more efficient and more humane than any that has gone before. But this promise and this challenge are lost sight of in the energy that goes and must go into making weapons of war. This energy has the real excuse that never before in history have free men faced the threat of a tyranny so large, so merciless and so painstaking as that with which the Soviet Union confronts us. Dangling between these two unique worlds – a world of unequalled slavery and a world of incomparable riches – we build the storm-cellars and hope for the best.

Most men find the problems of political power insoluble and tend to despair before a world that has shrunk in scale and enlarged in complexity, so that the knowledge of how it behaves seems more and more to be open only to the specialist. There never was a time, except perhaps in the fearful pestilences of the Middle Ages, when men hungered more for a decent private life, and when they are tempted to match in their joys the intensity of the sorrows all around them. I believe that this impulse, far from being an escape, is the only right way of asserting that human dignity which gives sense to the phrase 'an appetite for life'. What reasonable hope can an ordinary man have for himself and his family? Must we oscillate like crocodiles between panic and apathy? What more adult way is there of coming to terms with the alternatives of the atomic age?

I should like to have the wisdom and the knowledge to suggest something at once practical and noble. But all I can think of is an incident from the American past that comes nearer to home every day and seems to me as sensible as anything written since Hiroshima.

The time was the 19th of May, 1780. The place was Hartford, Connecticut. The day has gone down in New England history as a terrible foretaste of Judgement Day. For at noon the skies turned from blue to grey and by mid-afternoon had blackened over so densely that, in that religious age, men fell on their knees and begged a final blessing before the end came. The Connecticut House of Representatives was in session. And as some men fell down and others clamoured for an immediate adjournment, the Speaker of the House, one Colonel Davenport, came to his feet. He silenced them and said these words: 'The Day of Judgement is either approaching or it is not. If it is not, there is no cause for adjournment. If it is, I choose to be found doing my duty. I wish, therefore, that candles may be brought.'

Ladies and gentlemen, let candles be brought.

THE IMMIGRANT STRAIN

An item came over the news-tape the other day about somebody who wanted to organize a National Hobby Club. There is nothing earthshaking in this, but it opens up a field of speculation about Britons and Americans that I should like to graze around in. I saw this item and thought at once about an Englishman I know here, an old, old friend who – to be cold-blooded about it – has a value in this country over and above his value as a character and a good friend. I am, after all, a professional student of a rare species of goldfish – the goldfish being, you will guess, the American people. If you are a goldfish, or if you swim with them long enough, it is impossible to say what are the characteristics of goldfish. But if somebody drops a mackerel into the goldfish bowl, you can see at once all sorts of things that goldfish have and the other things they lack. That is why I am grateful to this English friend, just for being himself and for being around. He forms a stimulating point of comparison. He is a British government official in New York, and though I knew him for many years before he was sent here, I have lately learned many things about him I never knew and about Americans – the race he is at present moving among. For instance, when he comes into a room, one thought always strikes me, and I can say it two ways. I can say, 'Goodness, how short his coat is' or 'Goodness, how long everybody else's is'.

Now, in character – never mind his politics – he is conservative. He is an able and conscientious government official. He likes people and he likes to get through the day and attack in the evening his beloved hobbies, of which he has several. This characteristic alone would make him, in England, a typical civil servant. Here it makes him an oddity. He is a lepidopterist, an expert on moths. And when he was stationed in the Middle East he threw off what I believe to be an authoritative paper on the moths of Iran. Americans meeting him see his

17

black Homburg and his tight coat and his rumply collar, and hear his voice; and they know his type at once. They think they do. But they don't know it at all. If you feel baffled and alarmed at the prospect of differentiating one American type from another, you can take heart. You have more hope of success than Americans, who shuffle through every stereotype of every foreign culture as confidently as they handle the family's pack of cards. Americans are not particularly good at sensing the real elements of another people's culture. It helps them to approach foreigners with carefree warmth and an animated lack of misgiving. It also makes them, on the whole, poor administrators on foreign soil. They find it almost impossible to believe that poorer peoples, far from the Statue of Liberty, should not want in their heart of hearts to become Americans. If it should happen that America, in its new period of world power, comes to do what every other world power has done: if Americans should have to govern large numbers of foreigners, you must expect that Americans will be well hated before they are admired for themselves.

So Americans when they meet this Englishman for the first time at once file away the reflection that though he seems amiable enough, he is rigid, unimaginative, a little pompous, a regular Somerset Maugham colonial type. Then the telephone rings – as it did one night – and it turns out that someone wants to know who sang the vocal in that early Red Nichols record of 'Lazy River'. The Americans present were appalled and relieved to hear my friend give out reams of information on these matters. 'No,' he said to another query, 'I think you'll find that record is a blue label, and it's backed by 'Beale Street Blues', with Goodman and Teagarden ... What? no, no, the cornet is Jack's brother, Charlie – that's right, Charlie Teagarden. Not at all, so long.'

He is also, you gather, a jazz fan. And according to the late great Otis Ferguson he knew more about the history of recorded American jazz than most Americans alive, and wrote knowingly about it when he was in college, years before American intellectuals began to write jazz reviews in the middle thirties. I doubt if the Foreign Office know about this.

I doubt if they care, because he is an Englishman, and eccentricity is therefore the most normal thing about him. By merely being around he makes you notice how comparatively rare with Americans is an orderly set of hobbies; and how even rarer is the quality from which hobbies spring – namely, eccentricity. Active Americans do many things. And in different parts of the country they do routinely things that other parts of the country have never heard about. But by and large they do what other people, what their neighbours, do. There is a good reason for this, and you will be glad to hear we don't have to go back to the Indians for it.

Hobbies, I suggest, are essentially a tribal habit and appear most in a homogeneous nation. English boys in school sit beside other boys who are called Adams and Smith and Rendall and Barnes and Gibbs. They do not have to use up much of their competitive energy showing who is more English than another. A nation which says, 'It isn't done', is much more settled as a community than one which says, 'It's un-American'. Only thirty years ago Theodore Roosevelt made a campaign of urging immigrant Americans to forget their roots, to cease being 'hyphenated Americans'. But there are still in America two generations, the sons and grandsons of immigrants, who are trying to outlive the oddity of their family's ways. For it is a stigma for an American to talk with a foreign accent rather than with an American accent. This is snobbery, of course, but the people who instantly recognize it as such are enviably free from the problem. If it is snobbery, even in this land, it is a real humiliation: it is not the urge of insecure people to be different from others; it is the more pressing urge to be the same, and it is acutely felt among people who are insecure just because they *are* different. In very many American cities where there are large populations of immigrants, this is what happens: The son is, let us say, an Italian. As a boy he is brought up with a mixture of American and Italian habits. He plays baseball, but the big meal of the week is ravioli, and he is allowed little gulps of red wine. (If he is a Pole, he is dolled up once a year and marched in the parade on Pulaski Day.) Then he goes to school. There he mixes with boys called

Taylor and Smith and also with other boys called Schenck and Costello and O'Dwyer and Koshuski. He begins to find in time that ravioli is a mild joke at school.

Of course there are millions of Americans who eat ravioli who are not Italian-Americans, but they are untouched by the kind of problem I am discussing. Ravioli is an American dish by now. And that is another thing. The boy notices that just so much as his own habits and speech were instilled by his parents, by so much does he tend not to fit in. By so much he runs the risk of being a joke; which is no joke to a child. And then, at about the age of twelve, an awful thing happens. It is happening all over America all the time, and produces recrimination and heartbreak to the folks still left who came originally from the old country – from Poland or Italy or Czechoslovakia or Russia or Germany or wherever – and who will never master the American language. The boy notices that they speak with an accent. He never knew this before. But now it crowds in on him. Now he starts his own rebellion. And that is serious enough to many fine parents so that in scores, perhaps hundreds, of American cities the schools run night classes for parents, in the English language, to help them keep the affection and respect of their sons and daughters, or grandsons and granddaughters. It is a great theme in American life, and it cannot be dismissed by superficial horror or irritated appeals to decent feeling. In time, of course, masses of such sons and daughters outlive the threat of seeming different. And then, but only then, can they begin to cherish some of their oddity, especially in the way of food and festivals. Their strangeness becomes a grace note to the solid tune of their Americanism. But by that time they are sure of themselves and so able to look on their parents again – God help them – with affection.

So you see how sure of your standing with your companions you have to be to start, in boyhood, cooking up interests that will set you apart from your fellows. It will be no surprise now, I think, to hear from my Englishman that nearly all the members of his natural history club in New York were older men with Anglo-Saxon names – families that have been here for a hundred years or more, that have never felt anything but American. They start with the great advantage of being already

20

something that the Poles and the Germans and the Czechs and the Italians have to get to be the hard way.

You may wonder how an Englishman, and an English accent, fit into all this. Well, Englishmen who live here, no matter how long – first-generation Englishmen – are a special case. They may hope to be mistaken for Bostonians (but not by Bostonians). Yet if they affect any more Americanism than that which has grown into their characters, they do themselves much hurt, and both the country they came from and the country they adopted. There are Irish-Americans and Czech-Americans and Polish-Americans and German-Americans and Swedish-Americans and Italian-Americans and Greek-Americans. But there are only 'Englishmen in America'. They are always apart and always at once more foreign and more familiar.

And an English accent is by now just another foreign sound. There was a time when an English accent would take an Englishman into homes on the East Coast socially more elevated than the home he left behind him. Such Englishmen were secretly delighted to discover this while believing they were only being taken at their true worth. But the hosts knew better. This social observation was a favourite theme of American writers, New Englanders especially, in the early nineteenth century. Washington Irving once boiled over about a certain kind of British traveller: 'While Englishmen of philosophical spirit and cultivated minds have been sent from England to penetrate the deserts and to study the manners and customs of barbarous nations, it has been left to the broken-down tradesman, the scheming adventurer, the wandering mechanic, the Manchester and Birmingham agent, to be her oracles respecting America.' You can still run into the type. Or you could say more accurately that this attitude is one part of most Englishmen's character that is aroused by a visit to America. But the day is long past when Americans imitated English habits in order to be fashionable. There is, however, one peculiar hangover from that period. It is the convention of speaking English on the American stage. Unlike the British and the Germans, the Americans seem never to have worked out a type of stage speech true to the reality of the life around

21

them. Except in comedies. In most historical American plays, and plays of polite life, the characters talk a form of British English. If you chide Americans about this and say, correctly, that these people in real life would not talk at all like that, they say: 'Well, of course not; they're actors, aren't they?' I always feel in London that no matter how trivial the play, the characters being played would talk more or less that way in life. In this country it is understood as a convention, having nothing to do with social honesty, that actors should adopt an unreal mid-Atlantic lingo known, with a straight face, as Stage Standard. You may have noticed that even in American movies most American historical characters and members of Congress talk a form of British, while what are called 'character parts' talk American.

Englishmen can hardly be blamed if they assume that Americans share their sneaking belief that no American can be distinguished and yet sound American at the same time. It has given some otherwise shrewd English dramatic critics the idea that really educated Americans talk like Englishmen. The fact is that educated Southerners, New Yorkers, Chicagoans or New Englanders could never be mistaken for Britons. And there is something wrong if they could be mistaken for each other. It is a fairly safe rule that if in life you meet an American who sounds English, he is either a transplanted Englishman, or one of those homeless Americans forlornly bearing up under the 'advantages' of an education in Europe. Or he is a phoney. The American dramatic critic, Mr George Jean Nathan, was not intending to be facetious, but merely expressing a perennial American puzzle, when he wrote: 'After thirty years of theatregoing, I still can't make up my mind whether actors talk and behave like Englishmen or whether Englishmen talk and behave like actors.'

MY FIRST INDIAN

I have been reading the part of the late James Agate's *Ego* which has to do with his one and only visit to America. I know that Mr Agate was the kind of man so much in love with his own tastes in life that no two people will ever agree about him. But he was not a pallid man and he was not a hypocrite. What he liked he gloated over and so provoked rounds of applause in some readers and nausea in others. His section on America contains one completely objective statement, and like most objective remarks about nations it is a confession of what is most subjective in the onlooker. He notes that while sitting through an American stage farce he thought it was wonderful, but not in the way, and in the places, that the American audience thought it was wonderful. And he makes the honest comment: 'I feel I don't know these people any better than I know the Chinese. I felt painfully English throughout the entire farce.' I need hardly say that James Agate was the last man to be pained about *being* English, but here he hits off in a line the pathos that descends at some time on every traveller in a foreign country, however long or well he has come to know it: the sudden recognition that it is you, not they, who are foreign.

I agree with Mr Agate all the more because I was uprooted young, and laughed at this farce where the rest of the audience laughed, and am now so alien in London that I am baffled by British farces. In this instance, Mr Agate might have been writing about Abyssinia. But he had been honest for a moment about his bewilderment, and that is better – and more useful to later travellers – than the stubborn pretence of the visiting intelligentsia that intelligence is applied to much the same things in all countries, and that if you are bright enough you will be just as much at home with the humour of France or Britain or America. We have been having since the war ended a spate or rush of intellectuals, French and English mostly. I have read most of their subsequent books and articles and I can only say that any simple traveller who feels America will puzzle him has nothing to worry about. Nobody can be more comically stupid than a highbrow author professionally coming to grips with the 'truth' or the 'essence' of America. To get the feel of it takes long practice, a steady resistance to theories (other people's theories, that is); and when you have been here many years you will find that you still make elementary mistakes. Let me cheer you with an awful example from my own stumbling education.

About seventeen years ago I went to see my first Indian, what I then called a Red Indian. Like all comparatively recent visitors, I knew exactly where you looked for an Indian. Skyscrapers were in New York, waterfalls were at Niagara (nobody had ever told me there were a half-dozen as lofty in a single view over the Yosemite valley), fine buildings were in Washington, the countryside was called New England, and Indians were at Santa Fe.

I knew that Indians were at Santa Fe, because I had read D. H. Lawrence, who wrote powerful books about the Indian view of life. And he had gone to live in Santa Fe because he found there the particular escape he sought from the world he detested, the world of his own white skin. And he gave himself up to the Indian world, which – as I understood it – was a primitive, elemental sort of life in which people put their feet on the ground in a more down-to-earth way and in which men acted only on impulses that came from the pit of their stomach. As a young man who had been bowled over by Lawrence's writing, it was all very brooding and vital, far removed from the world I had known (and, being young, belittled) – of city streets, and working men, and seashores, and fishing from piers, and then college libraries, playing-fields, theatres, and people who wore summer dresses and business suits (the clods).

I took the Santa Fe train from Los Angeles and discovered, as everybody does, that it doesn't stop at Santa Fe. There is no station there. The Atchison, Topeka and Santa Fe Railway doesn't in fact touch Santa Fe, which if it were an English institution would be the reason it was so called. I got out at Albuquerque and took a bus sixty-odd miles north east to

Santa Fe, accompanied by two nuns and a Yale undergraduate who complained all the way that it was time that the British built some modern railway stations. The landscape was everything Lawrence had said it was. The evening was coming on and weird ramparts of cloud, of a gun-metal colour, cast forbidding shadows across the desert and the red mountains. There had been a shower of rain, quickly over, and up from the sage and the greasewood came that unique smell – a compound of peat and roses – that fixes forever in your memory the place where you first knew it. Nothing could be more satisfying to a romantic young man bred in cities than the semi-desert landscape that covers so much of the West. It is as empty as the horizon and gleams with splendid melancholy lights and haunting shapes. It is, as Balzac said in a famous short story, God with man left out. It was just the proper background to my reveries about the Indian. I knew before I'd seen him that the Indian was just what Lawrence had ordered. I got to Santa Fe and looked up the man who represented the government's Bureau of Indian Affairs. He was a small sallow man from Louisiana with rimless glasses and pop-eyes veined like the marbles we used to call 'bloods'.

Next morning we set off north in the direction of Taos, where Lawrence had lived. I was tense as a high C. But Mr Brown, the government man, seemed calm enough and I was horrified when he turned west on a dirt road at a sign pointing to something called Los Alamos. I would have been horrified for other reasons a dozen years later, for this was indeed the desert place where the first atomic bomb was exploded. These days its crater lies there outside a streamlined and well-guarded town of busy people making more atom bombs. Then and now Los Alamos gets up in the morning to the sunrise coming over the red peaks of a mountain range that lies to the east, and which bears the awful name of the Sangre de Cristo – the Blood of Christ range. But we were not going to Los Alamos. There was nothing there to see then. We were headed just short of it, to an Indian pueblo, which is what they call their little villages. The land was bared in a blinding light. Last night's brooding mountains were now as solid as crocodiles, red and purple crocodiles lying sullen in the heat. We came to the pueblo, a little cluster of mud houses shoulder high, and in the clearing that faced them were great half-spheres also made of mud, like huge beehives or, say, summer igloos. These were the Indian cooking-ovens.

We sought out the high priest, for he is the man who rules over the village. And I felt my pulse begin to thump. Here was I, a slim and possibly weedy-looking fugitive from the decadent life of cities. I too, like the white-skinned tourist villains in Lawrence, had come here not on the good steaming flesh of a horse but on the sweaty leather of an automobile. I had on a collar and tie. There was nothing I could do but tread a little more firmly 'deep from the ball of the foot into the earth', as Lawrence recommends, 'towards the earth's red centre, where these men belong'. The priest lived in one of these mud huts and had to bend low to come out of it. He was a big, copper-coloured man in blue jeans. He had long black hair knotted behind his neck. He had kindly black eyes and a face pitted and scarred like the Grand Canyon, where no doubt he was born. He asked us into his house, and I was proud to notice that whereas Mr Brown floated in upright from the sun into the darkness, I too had to stoop down and straighten up again inside. Inside was one room, the whole house. It had no furniture except a pallet against one wall. As we got used to the cool darkness I was curious to make out a pile of clothes up against another wall and shocked in time to see it turn into a woman. It was the priest's wife. She stayed squatting and smiled at us. Across the ceiling was strung diagonally a sagging double rope, which supported a hammock of dirty old clothes in which slept a baby. We admired the baby. The high priest bobbed. Then his grin vanished and he looked hard at the government agent.

'You brought them?' he asked in a deep, expectant voice.

'Sure thing,' said the Southerner and went out to the car and brought back three baseball bats, a catcher's glove and pads. The high priest gurgled over them and ran his big hand around a bat.

'Fine, fine,' he said, 'now everything okay.'

The Southerner said there'd be more if 'the boys' needed them. As we turned to leave, I noticed that one wall was entirely covered with what at first I had taken to be native art. Through the shadow odd dabs of colour had glowed, green and red and purple. I couldn't make out the form or sense of the mural. But I was impressed with it. Now high up in the middle of the wall I could recognize a tinted photograph of a painting of the Virgin Mary. It was a rotogravure supplement from a Los Angeles newspaper. The rest of the wall was covered with a row of colour photographs, torn from magazines, of automobiles. They were all of the same make of car. It was the priest's favourite make, and as he saw me squinting at them, he turned and, starting at the left-hand side with the designs of the early nineteen-hundreds, he trailed his finger across the whole mural, approving the brighter and flashier models with the ecstasy of a museum curator showing off his prize Egyptian pottery.

'Well,' said the Southerner, 'don't worry. You'll make it yet.'

The high priest laughed loud and bared his teeth. He beckoned us out and round behind his house. Standing there like a Roman emperor surveying the African desert was a vast open car, done in a blinding purple finish.

'What d'ya know!' yelled the Southerner, 'you *did* make it. Why, that's fine, just fine.'

We shook hands all round. The priest was bulging with pride. The Southerner shook his head enviously and we sauntered off. 'Great stuff,' he said, 'take it easy.'

'You take it easy, Mr Brown,' said the high priest.

We thanked him and waved good-bye.

On the way back – for I was sad to see that at the turn on to the main highway we went south again to Santa Fe instead of north to Taos – I thought it was time to bring up D. H. Lawrence. The Southerner looked straight ahead with a glazed sort of interest and seemed not to catch on. I wondered if there was a shrine to Lawrence up at Taos and he frowned a little. We drove on around little mesas and across great plateaus.

'Wait a minute,' he suddenly said, 'you wouldn't be talkin' about Lorenzo, would you – the painter?'

I remembered that Lawrence did paint and that he had at

sometime or other called himself Lorenzo. I said yes, I thought that was the man, though in England he was known best for his writing. I mentioned his essays about this part of the world, *Mornings in Mexico*, several of which were not about Mexico but New Mexico.

The Southerner sat intently at the wheel. 'No foolin'?' he said. There was a pause. 'A thin, red-headed fella with a beard, right?'

'That's the man,' I said.

'Well, now, I mean,' said the Southerner tolerantly. 'I reckon he had his livin' to make same as anybody else. That stuff he wrote, that sort of took care o' the butcher and baker. I mean you don't blame that fella, what's his name, for writin' about the Mediterranean. You know, spies and Mata Haris and all that sort o' theng.'

It was my turn to pick the missing author and in time I guessed right. E. Phillips Oppenheim was the name.

'That's the fella,' said the Southerner. 'Well, I reckon Lorenzo musta done the same kind o' theng with the Indians. If it paid fo' his supper, more power to him.'

There was, you can imagine, a terrific silence.

'Did you see where the President wants the gov'ment to start puttin' out some guidebooks about this country?' Mr Brown asked. But I saw only poor, great Lawrence thrashing in his grave.

ROUGHING IT

A hundred years ago the first ship sailed out of New York bound for San Francisco and the American River, where, according to the reports that had drifted East, you lowered a pan into a sluggish stream, shook it several times and sifted out a fortune in gold. By ship round the Horn was only one way, the most tedious and the safest. You could go by way of Panama and Nicaragua and run the risk of malaria or yellow fever. You could sail down to Mexico and face a shorter journey across its width through almost trackless desert and the chance of epidemics and slaughter by bandits.

Most people in the East who for one reason or another felt the urge to Go West decided to go the overland way. Today it is impossible to experience the human ordeal of that great migration, one of the last epics of purely human function before the Industrial Revolution transformed our lives. These people, in New England, and New York and Maryland and Ohio, sat down and planned to walk nearly two thousand miles from St Joseph, Missouri, or Independence, where the locomotive and the steamboat ended and the Middle Ages began. Independence was a more thriving place a century ago than it is today, because it was the outfitting centre for the Forty-Niners. From there you were on your own. You went by mule and drove your wagons and cattle along with you for the remaining eighteen hundred miles. You used a route map drawn by somebody who had once made it and survived. You depended very much, too much, on the hearsay of these people to know where the water-holes were and where you could take a short cut through the mountains.

There was no archetype of the Forty-Niner. They were of every human kind. But early on they learned that they had better travel in packs and most of them elected what they called a captain and two lieutenants. A quartermaster was chosen to look after the provisions. They may sound very martial in a noticeably non-military nation. But they knew, the later companies at any rate, that there were certain unavoidable hazards: flash floods, the rotting of their food, Indians, disease, and the constant challenge to their discipline and courage of reducing the weight of their pack – their implements, even their food supply – when the route was too much for their animals, who set the pace. They figured correctly that no group of human beings, however individually noble, would be likely to stay noble in the desperation of thirst, or spontaneously organize themselves in the event of attack. By the time they started the long journey from Missouri, most of them had formed themselves into companies and agreed on written or unwritten laws. Many of them spent weeks in the East before they left, drawing up written constitutions. Some of these were abided by all the way to California. Others were torn up in anger, stuffed down the captain's throat, or buried with a dead cow.

Most of them through the late spring of '49 took far too many provisions. It was said that the summer companies had the routes laid out for them by trails of abandoned stoves, pillows, beds, pots and kettles, crowbars, drills, ploughs, harness, trunks, bellows and dishpans. These, they found, were luxuries to a pioneer. And the word got across the continent that what you needed was one wagon to carry the supplies for every five persons, a mule apiece, rifles and shotguns, a rubber knapsack, an oilcloth cap, two pairs of boots, eight shirts, an overcoat, one pair of drawers, three blankets, a hundred and fifty pounds of flour, twenty-five pounds of bacon, fifteen pounds of coffee, twenty-five of sugar, some baking powder, salt and pepper.

That's as far as I want to go in describing the famous journeys across the plains. But I suspect that any American who started out today, fitted out just this way, and got to California, even if he stuck to the countless concrete highways that slam across hundreds of thousands of miles north and south and east and west – such a man would become some sort of national hero or crank. He would be paced by the newsreel boys, met at intervals by the advertising salesmen of whoever's flour and bacon he was carrying, he would be greeted by the

Mayor of San Francisco, he would in the end be flown to Washington and shown in all the papers shaking the President's hand in the White House.

Nothing persists more in the fancy of Europeans, and in the superstitious pride of Americans themselves, than the conviction that Americans are tough and rough and ready, scornful of the European niceties and primmer ways of travel. The last thirty years have turned this belief into unmitigated legend.

One of the most precious books to American book collectors is a copy of Baedeker's *United States* for, I believe, 1906. In the conscientious Baedeker way, it warns the comparatively domesticated European of the coarse pleasures and inconveniences he will have to settle for if he decides to take a holiday in the United States. It is always Baedeker's consolation, however, to the intending tourist that no matter how constant the public spitting, how hard the beds, how ankle-deep the roads and primitive the hotels away from the big cities, the traveller who has any pioneering spirit in him will never regret his courageous visit to the United States because nowhere else will he see the singing colour of the New England fall, the blossom of the South in spring, the grandeur of the Yosemite, the Yellowstone, etc., etc. This guidebook is greatly sought after precisely because today it reads like such a gorgeous joke. If you changed the place-names and made them European, an American could read it with a straight face, since it would record most of his grouches about travelling in Europe today. The application of American technical genius to the mechanics of living has not merely turned the tables on Baedeker, it has turned the American, however reckless or self-reliant his individual character, into the world's most urbanized, most petted traveller.

Mr Richard Neuberger, who lives in the Far West, in Portland, Oregon, has taken up this theme in a magazine piece. He was in Alaska during the war having, as he puts it, 'the sort of experience we had read about eagerly as boys, in the tales of James Fenimore Cooper, Jack London, and Zane Grey'. And, he adds, 'we hated it ... we talked nostalgically of percale sheets and fluffy towels, or breakfast in bed and tiled bathrooms'. They complained – in Alaska, this is – about 'draughty privies and the lack of dry-cleaning facilities'. Mr Neuberger concludes that 'with a few bold exceptions, we Americans have come to regard the steam-heated hotel and the internal combustion engine as indispensable to any foray in the open'. Nowadays, more millions than ever before (the latest published count was 29,608,318) visit the American National Parks. But according to the Department of the Interior fewer and fewer people each year attempt the two-day hikes, or even drive up the highest peaks, or, having looked at the Grand Canyon, will undertake the day-long mule journey down to the overnight camp at the bottom. It is very hard to say how Americans would compare with other peoples in this new-found lassitude. Driving around most of the National Parks is pretty strenuous in itself. If you could put Yosemite and Yellowstone together, you would have something about the area of Wales whose geography is a combination of Switzerland, Persia and the Day of Judgement. But even so, these parks were lovingly created two generations ago by men who chopped through thousands of feet of lumber, who rode into them on a horse, who discovered the sublime with an axe, a botanist's kit, a piece of bacon, a tent and a stout heart. Now through all of them, even over the hair-raising pass into Tuolumne Meadows on top of the Yosemite, American engineers have built incomparable cement highways, blasted through prehistoric rock, encircling mountains where no other race would dream of cutting out a dirt road.

This suggests a cheerful contradiction. That even if the traveller *is* a sissy sitting over an internal combustion engine, the heroes who in his behalf comb cement to the smoothness of toothpaste under the desert sun, and build his highways through the Rockies and Sierras: they are Americans too. And this leads us into a famous cliché. I hope I can then lead us out of it. (I have nothing against clichés. Most of them are true, though you have to live through the denial of them to know it.) It is the assumption that the Americans have grown soft and unable to fend for themselves, that their enslaving gadgets, through which they flip their way so expertly, are crutches or props to living, essential to a people sinking contentedly into a decadence that out-Romans the Romans.

I'm sorry to report that the Americans' devotion to urban comfort, their ingenuity with gadgets, even their reliance on them, proves no such thing. In my own experience, the Americans who are most devoted to convertible automobiles and glass-enclosed showers made no complaint on this score when they ripped up Japanese jungles for airfields or waded ashore at Okinawa. The women I know who can whip up a delicious meal in ten minutes with the skilled aid of pressure cookers, bean slicers, electric beaters and deep-frozen vegetables are also the ones who can make the best meal the slow way with none of these things. And the most skilful fisherman I know is a man who can charm a trout with his fingernail, but prefers to have a compact tackle-box along, which contains exquisite scales the size of your thumb and a leader cutter which is a little circle of plastic moulds that exudes fine wire and cuts it in one motion.

Most Americans, even rich ones, were brought up in a culture that never expected somebody else to do the rough work. Most boys in college who can afford good cars can also take them apart and put them together again. This may all be changing. Still, I doubt that a devotion to gadgets is a reflection in the American character of a terrified dependence on them. They are loved for themselves, for the humorous felicity with which they dispose of elementary labour. A Texan I know, whom I would never like to meet in anger whether the choice of weapons was a jet-propelled torpedo or the back of the raw hand, put it neatly once when he said to me, 'I'll ride fifty miles on a horse for the fun of it, but out of necessity I drive.' One of the irritating troubles about Americans, in violation of the best advice of the best English divines, is that they just don't believe that whatever is uncomfortable is good for the character.

WHAT'S THE MATTER
WITH AMERICA?

'The natives of England,' wrote an Italian ambassador to London about four and a half centuries ago, 'whenever they see a handsome foreigner, they say that he looks like an Englishman, and that it is a great pity he should not be an Englishman.' In England this remark has been quoted to prove the lamentable decline of Roman susceptibilities, since a thousand years earlier the observant Gregory the Great, looking for the first time on a shipment of Britons, had made the shrewder remark: 'Not Angles but angels.' This old reassurance drifted into my mind the other night when I heard over the radio an American senator, speaking from those cavernous lungs which the Almighty reserved for American senators, trumpet: 'I am an American – who is there in the whole wide world that does not envy the name?' Being in a defensive mood, I was reminded in turn of a Chinese general I met here in an army camp during the war. He had just been given a heart-warming account of the economic potential of China. He made a grateful little bow, and as the American general's arm went around his shoulder he remarked: 'Automobiles and cola drinks very good for Americans. But please, we should like remain Chinese.'

We were going into all this the other evening, a small group of about forty Americans who meet once a week to straighten the world out before the world goes to pot. The introductory speakers were two foreign newspapermen, a Hungarian and myself. We had been extended an endearing American invitation to come and say what was an American and, if we liked, to say what was wrong with America. It had been about fifteen years since I'd played this game, and I fumbled the better-known gambits. But the Hungarian had been here less than a year and was as impatient as a school chess champion.

He was a smooth, trenchant man in his early forties. In that room, where the amiable American bodies loped and leaned on chairs and tables, he was a very European figure. The creases of his double-breasted coat were horizontal, tugging at the unyielding buttons. He never unbuttoned that coat, as he faced an audience which, on a very hot night, was coatless. He had spent a lot of private time, he said, trying to find the word to define the dominant American character trait. He soon made it clear he had been pondering on a high ethical level, for he told us he wanted to find an equivalent for the three words which the Spanish philosopher Salvador de Madariaga had chosen to signify the dominant characteristics of the French, the Spanish and the English. These were: for the French – *droit*, which it appears is an untranslatable but enviable combination of justice, right, order and clarity. For the Spanish – 'honour', which we were given to understand was familiar enough but a passion with the Spanish people. For the English, need I say, 'fair play'. What, then, was the word for the Americans?

Everybody was deadly still. There was an audible purr from one end of the room, from two or three of the younger men who evidently join 'groups' in the expectation of hearing invited guests say the right things. I noticed a florid man near me, however, who flicked the ash off his cigar and gave me an ominous, ironical look that seemed to say, 'Well, boys, you asked him here.'

It will not surprise you, perhaps, to hear that the Hungarian had found the word. Somebody hinted later that he had known it before he ever took the boat across the Atlantic. The word was 'salesmanship'. His theory was that industrial genius is nothing in itself. Nor, it seemed, was there anything peculiarly American about a vast population of eager though slightly sceptical customers. It is the lifeline between them that counts. And that is the salesman. The product must connect with the buyer.

Elementary, maybe. But notice the snide American element in this familiar process. Where, he asked (and it must have been a rhetorical question, because he knew the answer all right), is the weakest link in the chain of supply and demand? Everybody waited politely and then let out an exploding gasp when he pronounced the word: 'the idiot'. The what? we

35

hissed and muttered. 'The idiot,' he said sternly. 'The intelligent man,' he explained, 'knows things the idiot does not know. But the idiot does not know some things the intelligent man does know. Therefore the idiot is the one who must be won over. At this point, the American system has to call on a body of shock troops who represent to American civilization what the Jesuits are to the Roman Catholic Church and the S S men were to the Nazis: the advertising men.'

There was a lovely bray of laughter, which horrified the Hungarian. 'You should not laugh at this,' he scolded. 'If you cried, that would be good.' Somebody motioned to show they were laughing with him, that he had a shrewd point, that no offence was meant, go ahead. But it did no good. The Hungarian had a theory, neat and sharp as a knife. And one could only wonder what, in his chagrin, he expected his audience to do about it. Most of us who get angry at another country do so in the absurd hope that the natives will squirm and hang their heads, confess and promise to reform. It is a childish mechanism, and the foreigner is always disappointed. An American doctor said to me afterwards that expatriates in any country always have to keep up a pet peeve against the system they find themselves in, to justify their inability or unwillingness to compete in that system. It is just possible that this was the wisest sentence of the evening, though it was spoken long after the meeting had broken up.

The Hungarian's main point was conceded in theory, and in courtesy. It was then demolished. An art director with an advertising company said sure, his aim was to sell his product, or his employer's product, but his layouts and designs were not aimed at the idiot. The daily zest of his work, he said, looking steadily at the table, was to paint striking and charming designs which would set up an unconscious preference for his product in just such wary and civilized people as the Hungarian. The man next to him said all business was a form of public relations and he thought it was a waste of character and talent if you didn't try to humanize it in every way possible. Another said he didn't get the implication that there was something shameful about selling things and that the Hungarian was gravely mistaken if he thought Americans were solemnly obsessed by it. 'I'd say,' this man concluded, 'it was more of a game and a matching of wits.' One melancholy man, whose leisure tastes ran to modern music and ballet, remarked: 'All the best cracks I ever heard about advertising were made by advertising men. But it doesn't make them throw up their jobs.'

All this was engrossing and good-tempered. But the meeting almost broke up in insurrection when I was called on to think aloud about the comparative significance of cricket and baseball. That afternoon I had been watching a baseball game between the New York Yankees and the Cleveland Indians. Early in the third inning a Yankee batter sent a high-fly ball soaring off, as we hoped, beyond the long white pole that marks the area between a foul and a home run. The umpire at first base whizzed around and craned his neck. The ball fell somewhere, and the spectators, being on the Yankees' home ground, roared their acceptance of the fact, which nobody had certified, that it was a homer. Then the umpire pointed this side of the pole and called a foul. He was right enough, but the crowd bellowed in pain and rage. So did the Yankee standing at first base. So did the batter. They both strode over to the umpire and spat out torrents of abuse. He cringed for a split second. Then his neck stiffened and he roared back at them. They squared their elbows back to demonstrate a merely technical respect for his person, but all the while they were shoving him along with their chests and he stumbled back under the rain of insult and calumny. The crowd loved this and egged on the three of them. When it was seen that the umpire and the players had taken over the crowd's indignation, the crisis dribbled away into waves of boos, laughter and rippling chuckles. It was a foul.

I mentioned this to our sweating group and wondered, possibly with too much coyness, why in a cricket game the first such word out of a batsman would have caused his captain to send him off the field. Somebody remembered that a marine in the south-west Pacific, very likely prompted by a newspaperman, had said that one reason the Americans were fighting the war was for the right to bawl out the umpire. This was too much for another Englishman present, who said that if an

English marine could have been got to express himself in a printable form about the common cause he 'might have said' he was fighting to have the rules respected. It was a glum moment. It appeared we had profoundly different ideas about elementary behaviour. What I was really trying to suggest, from the hideous bottom of my resentment at this baseball uproar, was that Americans were not very ethical about games. The other Englishman sensed the spot I was in and came in smartly to assure the company that cricket was a rather special case. The rules of soccer, now, are set up to be obeyed, but English soccer-players often express themselves, as he put it, 'very violently indeed'. (You mean, threw in the Hungarian, they go 'Hmmm!'?) At this point, we were in an untenable position. We were trying to prove the unprovable, namely that the British are very ethical but very virile at the same time. Our Hungarian magnanimously came to the rescue by harping again on his own more flexible theme. The Yankees, he thought, were simply using high-pressure salesmanship on the umpire. 'Salesmanship,' he snapped, 'leading to homicide.'

The evening ended triumphantly when a big swarthy man with large eyes and the bluest chin I have ever seen said in a tired way, 'Speaking as a Russian Jew, my good American blood boils.'

We all laughed with great relief and then, in the most patient and friendly way, he made several points that were received with general grunts of approval. He lit up just the difference, in a national attitude towards a game, that a proud Englishman might never understand and yet spend his life deploring. Every baseball player, he said, knows the umpire's word is law. But he's going to make the most of disputing it first. And the crowd expects a frequent show of indignation. Everybody knows it won't change the result. But it's a good show while it lasts and is included in the price of admission. One of the minor therapies of baseball, it seems, is to provide for the letting off of instinctive steam – or the national yen for anarchy. It has, he pronounced, very little to do with ethics.

There was one man present who was utterly and genuinely baffled by the news of an Englishman's strict fidelity to the umpire's little finger. The idea of a captain's ordering a player from the field because he had blasted the umpire to kingdom come struck him as extraordinarily prim and solemn.

'You mean,' he turned to me, 'they just wouldn't do it?'

'They just wouldn't do it,' I assured him down my nose.

'Tell me,' he asked, brightening, and the wrinkles vanished from his forehead, 'cricketers must be full of neuroses, right?'

It was getting very late.

'Right,' I said.

SOME OF OUR BEST CITIZENS

Willie Howard was one of those little, wistful men who –
like Chaplin, and Grock and the old George Formby – came
to great fame by keeping up the preposterous pretence of
playing the shrewd, debonair hero when it was obvious to
everybody looking on that this was the last part Nature ever
meant them to play. Willie Howard was sixty-two when he
died, and, since he started his career at the age of fourteen,
he spanned in his lifetime the rise and fall of the empire of
vaudeville. His was not so much an old-time talent as a talent
which expected an old-fashioned enjoyment of it. There is a
difference, a contrast which is wholly, I think, to our discredit.

The first newspaper I saw that headlined Willie Howard's
death made an unhappy coincidence of its choice of front-
page news. The main news was about one of the flare-ups
between Britain and Israel. It must have suggested a melancholy connection to many thousands of New Yorkers. It set
me thinking about the kind of comedian Willie Howard was.
I will tantalize you no longer. Willie Howard's real name was
not Willie Howard. It was Willie Levkowitz. And on the stage
he made endless, insane play with telling about his relations,
whom he regarded with a tolerant genealogical pride that
was wonderfully silly on a man who stood about five feet
three, whose body was no body but a dapper skeleton sur-
mounted with a flowing cape, a big drooping bow tie, and any
one of many black wigs that were meant to suggest an artistic
temperament but suggested merely a clearance sale of floor-
mops. 'My sister-in-law by husband once removed,' he would
announce, stroking his moustache the way he thought diplo-
mats stroke them. 'I have reference to Emmy Levkostein, née
Levkowitz.'

It would have been absurd to say that Willie Howard did
not enjoy making fun with Jewish names, and his New York
audience of thirty years ago would have thought you slightly

queer for bringing up the point. He was a Jewish comedian, who told Jewish jokes and also played many bizarre characters who were uproarious just because he was totally unfitted to play their prototypes in real life. 'The President of Mexico' was one. And for this he put on a moustache as wide as the horns of a longhorn steer, a sombrero that rested on the lobster claw that was his nose, and several assorted rugs that slithered to the floor during his presidential address, when he would pretend to be pained by the audience's giggles and go on in his serene ambassadorial style as he kept picking up the rugs and delicately put them on wrong again.

In speaking what he took to be Mexican-English, he would carefully and distinctly use Yiddish words and pause in alarm and bewilderment when the audience laughed. His most famous character was a French professor who gave language lessons. He would mince on – he had tiny hands and feet, and all his gestures were as delicate as Chaplin's, though he never seemed aware of it – he would come on, rap a huge cane for attention, wait till he got it and announce himself as Professor Pierre Ginsberg about to explain the peculiarities of what he called 'ze irrrrregulair vairbs'. He then spoke and taught a French that was no French at all, not a syllable of it, but sounded expert and idiomatic. He would rattle off a string of nonsense which ended with a bang on the word, pronounced in French, 'schlemihl'. Since in New York probably two-thirds of his audience were Jews – the Jews being great theatregoers – he was received with immediate warmth and understanding. I don't want to press the idea that his whole repertory depended on pronouncing foreign names in the accents of the Bronx. His most celebrated single act, which he'd been doing for thirty years, was the famous sextet from *Lucia*. Two queenly girls came on in evening gowns, led by three men in white tie and tails. They gathered together in an imposing concert group. The orchestra tuned up, and then Willie Howard came on in voluminous black trousers, a tail coat, a boiled shirt, but instead of a white evening tie, a long, long scarlet necktie. He joined the group and stood right next to one of the ladies, who was always chosen for her great height and her magnificent shape, or what we now call endowment. You will guess the mischief afoot if I simply report that Willie Howard came up to her chest. The orchestra played an introduction, which Willie Howard approved with many a condescending nod and wispy tracery of his hand. Then they began.

The first shock was that they were all very competent singers, including Willie Howard, who had a high, piercing alto, like a choirboy in hysteria. He would sing away with them, giving much sincerity to his performance with his candid, eager eyes, his great nose cleaving the air in time. In the interests of dramatic expression his face would duck slightly to the left, when he would see, exactly over the arc of his nose, and exactly at eye level, a vaster palpitating arc. It was the shapeliness of the blonde up next to him. His voice faded away, his lips fell apart, his eyes were full of a childlike, unsmiling wonder. He would stare beseechingly at the audience to see if it were really true. He would shrug his shoulders slowly and tear off into high C. I saw him do this nearly twenty years ago, and I saw him do it a month or two before he died. I hope they will let him do it in Heaven, for it was a performance of the pure in heart.

What you couldn't help but notice, in this and all his turns, especially if you were new to New York, was the absolute confidence and delight of his audience in these goings-on. The audience for vaudeville in most big American cities when it was in its prime was an audience of Jews and Irish and Germans and, in the Midwest, of Swedes. They expected to go and see comedians who were not merely funny men but were known, and often billed, as Irish comedians, Swedish comedians, German and Jewish comedians. An old-time vaudeville show was a racial free-for-all. To a new immigrant it was a time to get together, all barriers down, and stew in the broth of each other's failings and oddities. Of course, to let that happen, and to welcome it, you have to start with the unspoken conviction that different countries have different and laughable peculiarities. Jews especially have a family time with Jewish humour. And during one of the darkest periods of the Second World War, I for one was cheered and given hope by seeing a wartime audience let down its hair and its ideology and bask in the caricatures of Willie Howard and the intensely Jewish humour of Lou Holtz, who can keep apart in many a funny story the separate accents of Brooklyn, the Bronx and Manhattan's West Side.

Well, since the war there is less and less of this. Lou Holtz himself went on a radio programme and instantly got letters of protest calling him anti-Semitic. He put up a brave objection to this stupidity. But he and his kind can't win. There are more and more signs that we will no longer be allowed to admit in public the real and affectionate differences between one kind of American and another, outside the hearty regional stereotypes of the radio and the travel folders. A movie of *Oliver Twist* was banned in New York on the complaint that the portrayal of Fagin is anti-Semitic. A school board in Massachusetts has forbidden the reading of *The Merchant of Venice* in the public schools, because Shylock is represented 'in an unfavourable light', which is certainly the light Shakespeare meant to show him in. Little crass variations are creeping into old familiar songs, and these variations are becoming the official versions that have to be observed over the radio. The most pathetic I can recall offhand is a significant change in the lyrics of Jerome Kern's 'Old Man River'. In the play, you may remember, it was a Negro who sang:

> Niggers all work on the Mississippi,
> Niggers all work while the white folks play.

I don't know on what grounds this jingle has become unacceptable: whether it exaggerates a true but embarrassing fact, or whether it is, in the hypersensitive political climate of our day, a subversive (that is, a Communist) statement. Apparently, it is now indelicate even for a Negro to say – as he would say – 'Niggers'. So instead of 'Niggers all work on the Mississippi' it's now 'Folks all work on the Mississippi'. That leads to a little trouble in the next line. 'Niggers all work while the white folks play' has turned into 'Some folks work why-eyell some folks play'. Which, if you're going to get sociological about it, is a masterly bathos.

There are lots of other changes in the permissible lyrics of songs written in all innocence, often not more than twenty years ago. But many of these improvements are merely genteel. The ones that disturb me are the ones that have to do with different races, and ones which skimp the fact that Americans come from different countries and have different habits. Of course, it has been one of the great aims of the United States to turn strange peoples into Americans, but it can be argued that the American intention never was to deny the native characteristics but to modify them only so as to make it easier for everybody to live peaceably together in one big human family. It has been said that what is important in New York City is not the seething battleground of many races but the truce they observe.

The disappearance, then, of the Jewish comedian as such; the editing away of lines and thoughts in folk music that remind people of the special burdens of Negroes – these are defended as a move away from discrimination towards tolerance. But we seem to be using that word to blanket with good intentions problems that are far better uncovered and looked in the eye. To pretend that New York is not affected in its way of living, and in its opinion of foreign policy, by its two million Jews superficially looks like Christian charity but is in fact dangerous hypocrisy. It may well make us forget what we in New York owe to the Jews and to almost nobody else: the New York theatre, its music, the endowment of its fine libraries, the overwhelming Jewish contribution to psychiatry. It seems now as if we were moving into a period when the memory of what has recently been done to the Jews has made us want to overlook the fact that they are Jews at all. I suggest that this does them a disservice and in the long run will do great harm. When there is a gentleman's agreement not to bring up certain observed characteristics of a man or a nation, there follows from it the implication that those characteristics are necessarily unpleasant. If we scold children for making distinctions, we imply the guilty thought that the distinction is shocking. And I suspect that if we cannot, in politics and in our lighter moments, respect each other's differences; if we refuse to admit the peculiar good qualities of the Jews; we shall be in danger of forgetting the peculiar agonies they have suffered in our time and the special duty we owe them on that account.

A LONG ISLAND DUCK

I don't believe I ever told you about the duck that saved
two drowning people. It is not an unbearably alarming story.
And, to be entirely frank, the duck didn't really save anybody.
But it could have if it had wanted to.

To put it in its proper setting entails taking you down Long
Island in the late summer, a routine I had always thought of as
unspectacular until I had as a guest one time a friend from
California. He looked across our shimmering bay and took
on the wistful, hungry look that I get when I think of the
long morning light on the scarlet canyons of Utah or the
lupines carpeting the hills around San Francisco, which is his
home. Home, we decided, is the place you take for granted.
And as we sat tethered to the good earth only by a twenty-
yard fringe of chigger grass on a high sand dune, and watched
the blue bay frothing with little white caps from a south-west
wind, I confessed to him that if this were in California or
Oregon I would have written about it long ago.

The geography of Long Island is very easy to describe. It
is a flat fish lying north-cast of New York City, parallel with
the Connecticut shore. Its nose burrows into Manhattan and
its tail is a hundred miles out to sea, divided into two forks
or flukes as distinct as those on a tarpon or a Spanish
mackerel. Between these flukes lies Peconic Bay. We don't
think of it as a big island, or for that matter as a long one,
because it is nowhere more than about fifteen or twenty miles
wide, and a hundred and twenty miles is nothing very adven-
turous in a land where the motor car is the universal horse,
and where – once Mr Robert Moses had bullied enough imitation squires into selling the fringe of their estates – a system
of motor parkways was built which whisks you without a
traffic light through the first forty-five miles. You start out
from Manhattan and glide along the parkway and come out
an hour later near a place called Westbury. To your left, to-

wards the north shore, are impressive estates in the English manner, and Theodore Roosevelt's grave on Oyster Bay. A couple of miles south of the parkway is Walt Whitman's birthplace. It is a little shingled farmhouse that can be gone through any time between ten and six, but for the same reason that no New Yorkers ever seem to go up the Empire State building or the Statue of Liberty, I don't know anybody who summers on Long Island who has ever been to Whitman's old house. The same cannot be said about the Roosevelt Raceway, where there are trotting races every night. Anyway, these are places you read about in petrol-station maps and tourist guides. To anybody who loves the island they are merely arrows somewhere along a private journey signifying you are close by a favourite diner or seventy miles from your, from our, destination.

Very soon the island narrows in its middle, the fashionable estates thin out into potato and cauliflower farms, for that, as much as anything, is what Long Island lives by. Aside from the white cement beneath your wheels you will soon see the island much as it was seen by its first inhabitants, by the Algonquin and Peconic Indians, and then three hundred years ago by the few families from Suffolk who tried a winter in Connecticut, didn't like it very much and sailed across the Sound to land at Southold. Most of the names along the highway that runs down the backbone of the island are Indian and English names – Happauge and Nesconset, and Lake Ronkonkoma and Nissequogue, not far from King's Park, St James and Smithtown, where – as in a hundred places through New England – the grace of Sir Christopher Wren's signature has been written on wooden spires, on white churches slender as birches. You have another thirty miles or more to go before the island splits into its two flukes, one running south through the fashionable Hamptons to Montauk, an old whaling-station in the days of Moby Dick; and the north fork going thirty unfashionable miles through Polish country to Greenport, a fishing town settled by Yankees and Italians.

In this last stretch of the solid body of the island you go through nothing but farms, past roadside stands selling clams or corn, and then through scrub pine country so ragged after a long-forgotten forest fire that it looks like a piece of tundra that got shipped down by mistake from way north of Hudson's Bay. Along this stretch there used to be a sign saying, to Yaphank, to the place that was once unsentimentally known as the 'last stop' for Europe and the war to make the world safe for democracy. It was there that Irving Berlin wrote *I hate to get up in the morning*. In the Second World War it again became Camp Upton. And shortly after the war was over, the yellowing sign was taken away and they put up something very ominous: a sign saying, 'Right for Brookhaven National Laboratory'. It is a wide, paved road leading, it appears, nowhere through the aforementioned tundra to a high chimney on the horizon. This chimney was designed in its way to make the world even safer for democracy. But few chimneys can have started such a hullabaloo among the natives who live in sight of it. For Brookhaven is a national research laboratory for what are called atomic products. And the Italians, the Poles and the Yankees at the end of the island were smitten with an uncomfortable misgiving about what might happen to them and their issue if the radio-active wastes got airborne on a stiff south wind. The scientists put out reassurances that anything harmful to man or beast would thin out harmlessly long before it blew out of the top of the chimney. Just for goodwill, though, they built the chimney high. Some people have a hard time understanding atomic energy, and a tall chimney is an old-fashioned guarantee that what comes out high in the air will stay high.

By this time you are almost at Riverhead, and the moment we turn left to go up the north fork you can put your hand out and notice that the temperature has dropped from five to ten degrees. Peconic Bay is a fine thing to look at and fish in but it also is a cooling plant for the island's flukes. It cools off the warm winds and tempers the cold. Now you notice that the little white Colonial churches of the old English towns begin to alternate with heavy brown wooden churches that look as if they had a suspicious kinship with the Kremlin. This is the potato country, and it is farmed mostly by Poles. So that now you have the Anaskys living by the Hortons, the Ryskos selling groceries to the Glovers, in little villages that

47

run in the Anglo-Indian sequence: Aquebogue, Jamesport, Laurel, Mattituck and Cutchogue. Cutchogue is our town, and we go through it and turn down a two-mile peninsula that drops like a finger into the middle of the bay. On the end of it are sand dunes and a high bluff. And on the end of that am I, about to tell anybody still with me about the duck. There may be some misunderstanding if you have come with me so far, for one thing you would surely notice near Riverhead is a big duck farm, with nothing in sight but little willows by a stream lapping a small snowscape which, as you look at it closely, turns into several thousand ducks. They are the glory of Long Island, and once they are dead and eaten there is no satisfaction any more in ordering duck in a restaurant any-where else in the world. But the duck I have in mind was something else.

On this particular night in midsummer I drove home late and found my wife standing on the edge of the bluff looking through field-glasses out into the middle of the bay. We couldn't quite make out what it was. It could have been a small boat drifting on its side, or an abandoned raft. The thing that chilled our blood, though, was a small, probably improvised, white flag fluttering pitifully, no humans in sight. We tore back to the house and phoned the Coast Guard. Need I tell you that the Coast Guard, on the other shore, had barely heard of Peconic Bay, which is merely five miles wide and thirty miles long. They said they couldn't possibly come over from the South Shore and suggested we call another station at Center Moriches, a mere forty miles down the island. We phoned them, and an alert, Clark Gable guttural said, 'Yes, ma'am, we'll be right over.'

We waited miserably for three-quarters of an hour or more. We have a quick twilight and in the end we lost sight even of the white flag. Then from behind the dunes lights swung into the sky, there was a peeping and roaring of motors, and suddenly a whole cavalcade of cars and jeeps, and station wagons and camp followers came clattering along behind the man with the duck. A duck, I should explain for those who were not in the amphibious forces, is like nothing that ever was, before the last war, on land or sea. The current model is a monster automobile about the length of two American trucks; its superstructure is a gleaming lifeboat. We could hardly see the pin-head of the driver and two of his lieutenants bobbing up at the top. They were, you understand, at the end of the road. Ten feet in front of them was scrub pine and sand-dunes and then the dark waters of the bay. We waved frantic directions at them, told them it was round the other end of the point.

Before our chattering group could catch its breath, the duck chugged and roared and ran forward, crushed the scrub pine, keeled over the sand-bank, slithered along the soft sand, paused to disinflate its tyres and with a prouder roar went thundering out into the bay with its headlights raking the water. It sloshed up to the raft or boat or whatever like a Great Dane nosing around a Pekinese. It turned almost at once, plunged back to the shore, made the same split-second pause to reinflate its tyres, dredged through the sand again, roared up the bank and over the smothered pines, and paused growling at our feet.

It turned out to have been a marker-buoy for a yacht race the next day. The yacht club had evidently forgotten to report its location to the Coast Guard.

The captain, or the man from Mars, or whoever drove the duck, leaned over the looming top. A hard eye gleamed through the darkness. He was obviously a veteran of Okinawa, or a twenty-five-missions-over-Germany man. 'Who,' he shouted, 'reported this — accident?'

My wife sidled forward. She is, or was at that moment, just going into her teens.

'I did,' she said. 'I'm awful sorry.'

The airborne eyes melted and we saw a flash of teeth.

'That's okay,' the voice said. 'We've been sittin' around chewing our nails for weeks hopin' somebody'd let us try out this gadget. Some stuff, eh?' He grinned and the engine roared again. And it crashed off into the night, followed by the jeeps and the cars and the station wagons, and all their occupants, delirious and purged as little boys. Which, as everybody knows, Americans are.

DAMON RUNYON'S AMERICA

When Damon Runyon died the papers were black with columns of sentimental farewell from all the New York sportswriters who possess an expanding waistline and a yearning to break with the daily grind of football and the horses and begin to write some profitable short stories on the Runyon model. He is already becoming sweetened into a legend, and it sometimes does take the death of a man who summed up an era or a fashion to make you feel how dead and done with that era is. But Runyon has a peculiar transatlantic interest, because the people who read him in London were not the people who read and admired him here. His English reputation, among highbrows especially, was one of those puzzles that are politely accepted as insoluble by the Americans who run into them. It produced the same sort of shock to cross the Channel and hear intense French intellectuals sneering at the talents of Jean Gabin and Louis Jouvet and wishing the serious French *cinéma* could achieve the *vitalisme* of Jimmy Cagney or 'this tenderness, cynical yet profound' of Humphrey Bogart.

Maybe you are both right. But let us for once go beyond politeness and look into the life and style of a man who, by some trick of understanding or misunderstanding, seemed to a whole generation of Britons to be the most typical American writer of his day: tricky, racy, pungent, slick, amoral. I'd better say at once that I never met an American, unless he was a Broadway nightclub owner, or a racing tout, who took that view of Runyon. And the only intriguing thing about him to many literate Americans was his great reputation in Britain.

Like so many other people who later become identified with the spirit of the place they write about, Runyon was not born there. In fact he was twenty-seven before he ever hit New York. He was born, by a funny coincidence, in Manhattan, but Manhattan, Kansas, which in 1884 must have had a population of several hundreds. Runyon's father was an itinerant printer in the Midwest and West. Runyon followed his father, and it took him through a pioneer's trail of Kansas towns, from Manhattan to Clay Center to Wellington, and finally to Pueblo, Colorado, a small town, not much more than a run-down Indian village, just near what is now the Mesa Verde National Park, where you can see the towns built in the sides of cliffs by Indians whose high civilization crumbled about nine centuries ago. It seems to this day a very unlikely place to set the imagination agog with the 'dolls' and 'characters' of Runyon's imagination.

Young Runyon at fourteen ran away to enlist in the Spanish–American war. He was in and out of guerrilla war-fare for two years in the Philippines, and came back to Colorado full of tall stories, a tobacco breath, and a trick or two with a poker deck that qualified him at once for the profes-sion of newspaperman. By now his interests were settling into the groove that was to pay off very profitably in later life. He started baseball clubs, ran boxing matches on the side, and rode horses on small tracks in southern Colorado. It would be tempting to add that here he obviously picked up the authentic lingo of baseball and stables, and of the petty gangster and shill and the like. Maybe he did, but again like other writers who have been acclaimed outside their own country for their accurate ways with the spoken language, Runyon was not then or ever later a particularly good writer of American idiom as she is spoke and writ. I would say, and it's not an eccentric opinion, that he could not begin to hold a candle to Westbrook Pegler, or John O'Hara, or the late Otis Ferguson, or the living Red Smith, Jimmy Cannon, John Crosby or Robert Ruark. Some of you may be waiting for the name of Ernest Heming-way. But he would come into this discussion only because he too writes an American idiom that no American has ever spoken. It is the American vernacular heard through a very personal ear-trumpet. The Americans in Hemingway talk more like Hemingway than Americans, but somehow they couldn't be anything else but Americans and Hemingway characters. He tightens their speech and their emotions, like a man over-tuning a six-string guitar, so that the low notes have a sharper twang than they ought and the high notes sound as if they were struck on an icicle.

Damon Runyon, even back in Colorado, must have had some trick of mind and hearing much as a man with terrific astigmatism sees distant objects, in a queer way that makes the vertical lines jarring, but also more exciting than they are when he puts his glasses on. I speak with feeling about this because I am a four-star veteran of the battle with astigmatism. I remember how, at my first dances as a boy, when I didn't know there was anything wrong with my eyes, I'd look across the ballroom floor and see a whole crop of misty, tender wallflowers swooning on the vine. I would slink madly round the edge of the dancers to grab one of these houris for my very own. However, when I came within three feet of the charmer I had singled out to tread on, I saw at once why she was a wallflower, instead of being, say, Ava Gardner, out there on the floor moving like a snowflake, or – to be frank – doing the Charleston. When I got close she was rarely a beauty, though she looked human enough and surely had character; but that is unfortunately not what a fifteen-year-old is looking for in girls. I used to take a quick, mild dislike to these girls, however, because they seemed to have pulled a Jekyll-and-Hyde trick. I discovered from some patient clinical testing later that this is the characteristic deceit of astigmatism. Almost any attractive woman at thirty yards looks to me like a beauty, because the astigmatic gaze softens the hard vertical lines, irons out all the wrinkles, and turns any deep-set pair of eyes into pits of tenderness. In general, the great gift of astigmatism is to rob a face of its peculiar lapses from the ideal and leave you with the Platonic copy of the girl that is laid up in heaven.

That's the way I think it was with Damon Runyon. He first saw New York from afar, and heard about it from the lips of gamblers and soldiers and race-track touts who had made a haul there, or gone on an immortal bust, or captured some fabulous 'doll'. He swam into New York through the romantic haze of his astigmatism, put his glasses on, liked the Colorado myth a good deal better, and kept his glasses off. He didn't care to put them on again, because he did very nicely selling

America and Europe a romantic commodity easy to recognize at a distance. He didn't need, either, to listen for Broadway's slang. The private circus in his mind's eye had a lingo all its own, and he made it up as he went along.

A character in a movie Runyon once wrote called somebody a 'mooley'. The censors wouldn't pass the movie till they'd checked with Runyon. 'What's a mooley?' they asked him nervously. 'A mooley?' he said. 'Why, I don't know, I made it up.' That's the way with nearly all his slang. Most American slang was never made up by writers. It derives from a long American experience of work or play – from the collision of Dutch and French and German with English, or from the Spanish days of the South-west, or from pioneering, mule-driving, railroading, baseball, poker, the cattle kingdom, mining. A newspaperman famous for his exposures of corruption in labour politics said to me the other night that he thought he might soon turn his attention to the rackets that go on in the insurance business. Reflectively he said, 'I think I'll sink a pick in it. Might be some pay-dirt there.' That is authentic and natural. There is no such slang phrase current as 'to sink a pick'. But I guess it was a common working expression seventy years ago. It recalls at once the Western miners, who looked at a likely mountain range, spat on their hands and sank their picks in, and came up, some of them, with a fortune in silver.

On the contrary, Damon Runyon's slang is as contrived and romantic as Dickens, as synthetic as Broadway. Perhaps that's why it fits, even though Broadway doesn't talk it. If Broadway characters had a vein of crazy property, they might talk that way.

Runyon as a writer never goes as deep as Ring Lardner, and his irony was superficial enough not to sadden him with the knowledge of human meanness and vulgarity, as it did Lardner. Runyon accepted it and was fond of it, which might make him a healthier man and not so good a writer as Lardner. He saw, as a stranger, one very small and flashy section of New York life. He made it over into a puppet world of his own, where gangsters are lovable bums, and greed and vulgarity are fun and hurt nobody – for long. He was able to do this because he preserved and exploited his original innocence, like a certain kind of confidence-man. The British view of Runyon is as confident and odd as Runyon's view of New York, not so much because distance, like astigmatism, lends enchantment, but because Runyon distils and sterilizes for a foreigner the swarming colour and frightening behaviour of the animals known as New Yorkers. All the most popular comic writers deal with some recognizable place, and then flatter your foreignness by letting you in on the secret, the confidential, the positively gen-u-ine low life of the place. So Damon Runyon saves you the expense of the voyage, the very real puzzles of the real thing. He puts you in the know, and the knowledge is a cure in itself because it gets you away from the daily grind and the recognizable life of Leeds or Glasgow or London – or, I ought to add, New York.

You do not have to be a stranger to describe or enjoy this pleasurable and simplified view of the country or a town. I know a wealthy tycoon who now lives in New York. But he started life out West, as a timekeeper with a railroad gang. He has acquired without pain, in later life, a romantic Eastern view of the West, thus throwing into reverse the imaginative mechanism of Damon Runyon. This man is always asking me to come and visit him at his winter home in Arizona. Great country, he says, great people, great life. I mumble something about having work to do. At my age, he too had work to do. But now he goes off before the January snows and comes back in April, when the trees are blossoming. He has taken on a stranger's view of the West that is large, enraptured and sentimental. I thought of his father, who had no view of the West, but just broke it and made it liveable.

I have meant not to answer but only to ask the big question: can anybody ever know what is typical of another country? Is Lawrence's Arabia really Arabia, or only what Lawrence's gallant and secret imagination wanted it to be? Would Byron's poems on Greece have made a Greek laugh, as the English editions of Runyon make Americans laugh, with their glossaries of what the English editor thinks is American slang? We are up against a great and humbling question. And the only consolation I can offer is that the answer is open to anybody, the field is free. I have noticed that insight into American ways has nothing much to do with intellect or education. Most people find in a foreign country what they want to find. And when it comes to handing out the laurels to another nation's writers, the native critics are only the muscle-bound trainers of the day. They have been wrong before. If you go back into the last two centuries and look over their selections of the living immortals, you will be given faith in your own fumbling hunches. And even though we on this side may shudder at the notion that you think we go around talking like Damon Runyon's characters, maybe you are right about his permanent fame. After all, you have been right before, notably about Mark Twain, when all the best people in America, and the most respected critics, considered him something as low and fleeting as a comic strip. Maybe Damon Runyon *has* created a legend more enduring and endurable than the reality, because it is neater and funnier and more exotic and sympathetic – that is to say, more artistic – than crummy, sluttish old Broadway could ever be.

JOE LOUIS

The day Joe Louis retired must have brought a moment's pause and a sigh from many people who don't care for sport, the sense of a promised date that would never be kept such as non-musical people felt when Caruso or Paderewski died. On the 1st of March, 1949, it came home to some of us that we should very likely never again see him shuffle with great grace up to some wheezing hulk of a man, bait him with a long left before he brought up the shattering, awful thunderbolt of his right, and then toddle considerately away and wait for the referee to call the roll on yet another ruined reputation.

There are some idols you acquire too early, who later turn into walking parodies of themselves, like a favourite uncle who gets to be a vaudeville bore. There are others – the artists of popularity – who stay just far enough away from the hungry crowd and never glut the appetite they tease. Joe Louis was one of these. I doubt I should ever have seen him, or cared to, if he had not at one time connected with a private occasion. I went down to Baltimore the first day of summer in 1937 to stay with an old friend, a doctor at the Johns Hopkins hospital, who promised himself next day an afternoon off from his messy labours with stomach-aches and corpses. We drove out into the blossoming Worthington and Green Spring valleys. The purple twilight fell. It had been a perfect day, of the kind that makes you grateful for your friendships and stirs the memory of how they first started. I had met this man years before on such an evening when he stopped by my room in college to admire a battered record I had carried across the Atlantic. It was Fats Waller singing the *Dallas Blues*. Driving back into Baltimore he remembered that Fats was on tap in person just then. 'How about,' he said, 'we go down to darktown and catch him?' There was a little vaudeville house deep in the coloured section of town, and that's where we went. We packed ourselves in with several hundred Negroes too many. They clapped and stomped in time and sweated like the plebs at a Roman circus. It was possibly ninety-five degrees outdoors and a hundred and ten inside. Nobody seemed to care. In the middle of one number, though, something happened outside that rode above the rhythm of the band and the hallelujahs of the audience. Far off from somewhere came a high roar like a tidal wave. The band looked uneasy but played on. It came on nearer, a great sighing and cheering. Suddenly there was a noise of doors splintering and cops barking and women screaming and men going down grabbing their toes and snarling obscenities. The band stopped and the lights went up. The black faces all around us bobbed and flashed. Women threw their heads back and shrieked at the roof. Some people embraced each other and a little girl in pigtails cried. Other people cuffed and swung at each other. We managed to get out whole. Outside, in the villainously lit streets – they still have gaslight in darktown Baltimore – it was like Christmas Eve in darkest Africa. This, it turned out, was the night that Joe Louis won the heavy-weight championship, and for one night, in all the lurid darktowns of America, the black man was king.

The memory of that night has terrified and exhilarated me ever since. The phrase, 'Arise, you have nothing to lose but your chains', must have a terrible appeal to the Negro. Most Southerners know it, and it is why in some places they watch fearfully for every Negro flexing his muscles and wonder if he is somehow connected with the Communists. That immediate fear was not besetting America then as it is now. But the lesson was plain: one Negro had outboxed all the living contenders, no matter how white (and Braddock was whiter when he came out of the ring than when he went in), and he was a racial god.

It took several years, and a run of inevitable victories, and wide familiarity with Joe in the ring and on the newsreels, for Americans to learn a special respect for this quiet, beautiful, mannerly youth, who never thought of himself as anybody's god, who never played his colour up or down, kept his mind on his work, stepped scrupulously aside when an opponent stumbled; and who, when it was all over, said such embarrassing things over the radio that they had to whisk the mike away from him to the loser, who could usually be depended on to say the clichés that were expected of him. They pushed the microphone up to Joe in December, 1947, when he had been fought into a dazed parody of his younger self by another old Joe – Jersey Joe Walcott. A sharp little announcer chattered, 'Did he ever have you worried, Joe – at any time?' This is a question expecting the answer, 'No, I felt fine all the time, never better.' Joe said, 'I was worried all the way through. Yes, sir, I ain't twenty-three any more.'

I know it is hard, perhaps impossible, for any white man to appraise the character of any Negro. If you have lived all your life around Negroes, you inherit certain attitudes towards them. If you are a stranger to them, there is the danger of making them out to be quite the nicest people in America. In a way, nice Negroes have to be; for though Negroes are as good and bad as anybody else, they have one thing in common: they have had, most of them, a worse deal than the white man. A variation of this condescension is to think so poorly of the Negro in general that when he does anything as well as a white man, you have to make him out to be unique. You hear a coloured band and shout that nobody can play a trumpet like a black man (it depends, of course, which black man is being compared with which white). Then you run into Louis Armstrong, who tells you of the first time he heard a white boy – a very pasty-faced boy from Davenport, Iowa – play the cornet. And Armstrong broke into tears. 'Man!' he said, 'might as well lay you down and die, nigger.'

When you come to look at the life and career of Joe Louis, there is the special dilemma that he is a black man, and that even when you have done your best to judge him as other men, there's no way of denying that if he is not the best boxer that ever lived, he is as near to it as we are ever likely to know. He was born in 1914 on a sharecropper's cotton patch in Alabama and was as country-poor as it is possible to be. In theory the farm was – it had been rented as – a cotton and vegetable farm. But the vegetables did not feed the family, not by the time Joe, the seventh child, came along. His father broke, as sharecroppers do, from the daily strain of not making enough in crops either to feed his children or put shoes on them. They had no money to send him to a hospital. So he was carried off to a State institution where he died. A widower came to help out and soon married Joe's mother. And his five children moved in with the eight Louises. Joe got a little more food and went to a one-room school. Then the family moved to Detroit, where the stepfather worked in an automobile factory. Joe went on to trade school and worked in the evenings doing the rounds with an ice-wagon. Then came the depression, and the family went on relief. This, said Joe, made his mother feel very bad. Years later Joe wrote out a careful cheque for two hundred and sixty-nine dollars, which was the amount of the relief cheques they had had from the government. That, said Joe, made Mrs Brooks, as she now was, feel better.

Whatever a big city means to the poor, Detroit meant to Joe. But it means something else to a hefty Negro lad short of cash. It means gymnasiums and the prospect of a quick take of two or three dollars in improvised fights. When Joe was eighteen he came home very late one night and found his stepfather blocking the door. 'Where you been, Joe?' he asked.

'Over to the gym,' said Joe, 'working out.'

'I thought so,' said Mr Brooks and lectured him about the fate of no-goods getting punch-drunk in gymnasiums. 'You go on foolin' around with boxing, you're never gonna amount to nothin'.'

He says this had him really worried. He asked his mother about it. She said it was all right to be a boxer if that's what you wanted to do most. And that was, in a way, the end of Joe's wayward life. The rest was practice, and workouts, and learning, learning, being knocked to pulp, and learning some more and coming again with a new trick or two.

There is a biography of Joe Louis, there may be several, that makes him talk the way sentimental writers always think simple men talk. It is a fairly nauseating work. But just before Joe retired two first-rate newspapermen, Meyer Berger and Barney Negler, got hold of him for many long sessions and, presumably with one hand in their pockets, transcribed exactly how he talked and what he said, without paying any more attention than Joe Louis does to grammar, simplicity or morals. From a few sentences of this report, I think you can get closer to the sort of man Louis is than from reams of official biographies. Take the bit about his being born with a catlike tread. 'When I got up in fighting,' he says, 'newspaper writers put a lot of words in my mouth. They wrote I was born with movements like a panther, and how I was a born killer. I never said it was wrong before, but the real truth is I was born kind of clumsy-footed. My mother says I liked to stumble a lot when I was a baby ... That footwork the writers say was cat-sense was something Chappie Blackburn drilled into me. That was learned, it wasn't a born thing. He saw I couldn't follow my left hook with a right cross without gettin' my right foot off the floor. It takes a lot of learnin' before you can do it without thinkin'.' Or his explanation of why he never says much. 'When I got to be champion, the writers made a lot of noise about how hard it was to get me to talk. My mother said I was no different when I was a kid. When I went to school the teacher made me say words over and over and by-and-by I got stubborn, I guess, and wouldn't say them at all.'

After he lost a fight in early 1934, before his professional career was technically on the books, his manager told him to stop staying out late with the gang. 'He treated me real good,' says Joe. 'I got to wear some of his clothes made over.' The night he became champion, the night it seemed the whole population of darktown Baltimore poured into that vaudeville theatre, Joe summed up his feelings in an immortal sentence or two:

'He fell in a face-down dive. That made me heavy-weight champion. People figure that was my biggest thrill. But I don't remember no special feelin', I just felt good ... maybe it was because I figured I wouldn't feel a real champ until I got that Schmeling. That's what I fixed on.' (Schmeling it was who rang the only jarring note on Joe's professional record. At the end, it read: 61 bouts, 15 knockouts, 9 decisions, knocked out once. That was in 1936. And exactly one year to the night after he became champion, Joe had his revenge. He did what he 'fixed on'.)

Maybe you will get from this the idea that Joe Louis is a simple soul with quiet manners, a good boy who never had a crafty thought. Of course, he doesn't talk about his respect for his opponents, or his decency and casualness with the crowd, because these are fundamental, the characteristics that a man hardly knows about, or, if he does, keeps quiet about. But there is one remark he makes about his pride in money that should round out the picture. 'People ask me,' he says, ' "Joe, what will you do when the big money from fightin' stops comin' in? Won't you have to cut down?" I tell 'em, I'm gonna live good, retired or not retired. I got investments and I got ideas. I'll keep on livin' good. It's them who lived off me who won't be livin' so good.'

Well, there he is, the Brown Bomber no more, a memory of incredible speed, a slow shuffle, a solemn face, a gentleness, a shy acceptance of his greatness. All things considered, a credit to his race. So long as you add Jimmy Cannon's necessary afterthought – the human race, that is.

A BIG SHOT

What makes a big shot? How does a private man turn into a
public character? Why are Americans so direct and easy when
they are anonymous, and so pompous and self-conscious when
they turn into celebrities?

These are not my questions. They are the challenges put up
to me by a correspondent. They are pretty sweeping judge-
ments masquerading as a cry from the heart. I doubt that
American big shots are more or less offensive than others.
The accusing word 'pompous' would certainly puzzle Americans. They think of themselves as being, more than anything,
natural and unpretentious. But all these words are abstract
words, and they mean nothing until they are filled with the
colour that different languages give them. The Frenchman's
idea of what is natural is not like the American's or the Englishman's. Most nations associate 'pompousness' with the English character, especially if they dislike it. Of course, they are
insane. Still, many an English spy has made the disturbing
discovery that very little pomp, of the English sort, goes a
long way abroad, especially among the Latin nations, so that
a man who is thought pompous in America may be classified
as a mouse at home. What is dignity? or formality? or
humour? or beauty in men and women? or rudeness? or
courtesy? There is no universal understanding of these things,
and the British and Americans would by no means agree about
them. They might agree on a definition, but they would not
agree when the definition took flesh and went into action.
The Americans think that the British idea of a formal occasion
is something very formal indeed. But Britons can never get
used to a supposedly informal people who call a dinner a
'banquet' and who spend ten minutes with another man and
call it being 'in conference'; and who, when their father dies,
seriously say that he has 'passed away'.

The British and Americans suffer from a common difficulty which confuses also the relations of the Brazilians and the Portuguese: they share a language. Whenever you catch yourself trying to distinguish American and British qualities by using abstract nouns, you might recall that whereas a Briton believes that an American was born talking British and then was transferred to the Bronx, an American believes that an Englishman was born talking American but was put on stilts at an early age. A Californian friend of mine, on his first visit to Britain, marvelled at the accents of shopkeepers and bank clerks and lawyers and all women. Children, of course, were not to be believed. They sounded to him more precocious than French children. He got used to British in time and could credit its being a form of speech taught in the cradle. But the women defeated him. 'What,' he asked me, 'do they talk in bed?'

Having cleared the ground a little, or possibly cluttered it up, I can now go on to try to answer my correspondent's question about the transformation of an amiable American into a monster by the unexplained process of becoming 'a big shot'. I don't think I have the answer, but I have watched the process several times. And I shall tell one history, and hope the correspondent will find his own answer; he may conclude that in this country the steady application of organized publicity and press-agentry is responsible for more lapses from original innocence than the apple and the serpent.

In the early part of the war, I had a friend working in the government. He was a brilliant man, which is not a rare thing, but a brilliant man who was also kindly and warm-hearted, which is. His chief in government work was an ageing politician who'd been famous enough in his own state but who had never been more than a local visitor to Washington. This old man was suddenly called by President Roosevelt to one of the highest offices in the American government. He was confirmed by the Senate. And although when he arrived he never knew where to hang his coat, within the week he was installed in a big office with glossy leather chairs, gleaming floors and files, a brace of secretaries and an outer waiting-room. My friend was at once attached to him to show him the ropes of his department.

In a city which exists for government and nothing else, which works at politics by day and talks it by night, and which cooks the most natural ideas in our language into an indigestible jargon, this old man had a directness, a shambling friendliness, a whimsicality which you could meet up with almost anywhere else on a golf-course, in a fishing village, on a farm. My friend's first problem was to protect this old man from himself, to stop him letting his waiting-room become a hang-out for busybodies, lobbyists and old acquaintances on the make. When this was done the next thing was to teach him to be aware that, as a spokesman for an American policy that was of anxious concern to America's allies, he couldn't be quite so free with his anecdotes in public as he was accustomed to be.

Now this old man was in the news every day. He had a regular press conference, which was great fun at the start. He was the chief speaker at glittering dinners. He was required to troop through airplane factories and pause before B-29s and give them that distinguished thoughtful look which often makes you wonder if, left to himself, the man would know how to ride a bicycle or change an electric-light bulb.

By this time, my friend was running into serious trouble. Articles, sketches, profiles of the grand old man began to appear in national magazines, and his character was stream-lined and doctored – quite unknowingly by the journalists, of course – until you had only to see a couple of adjectives before a name to know at once what name would follow. 'Wily, down-to-earth' was one favourite combination. Another story at the time started, 'Last week, the Department of So-and-So's massive, shrewd commander-in-chief ...' And sometimes you'd have a resounding little clause after his name, as in, 'An unholy row was brewing in the Department of So-and-So late last Friday. Impatient juniors padded up and down the outer office of their wily, massive old chief. But the chief, nobody's fool, had gone fishing.'

Now, everybody is somebody's fool, if only his wife's. And

the old man was not massive; he was not wily, he was shrewd, and he had never before been told that he was down-to-earth. This was his undoing. At some private time, shaving his right cheek perhaps, he must have said to himself, 'Come to think of it, I *am* down-to-earth, at that.' Of course, he didn't need to stop and doubt it. Have you ever met a man or woman who didn't think they were shrewd? It's an assumption everybody makes, like having a sense of humour; though if we all had humour, there would be no such thing, there'd be nothing to laugh at.

In short, the old man began to live out the character the magazines had given him. He was not aware of it. His amiable habit of being all things to all men made him begin to be deliberately off-hand with everybody. To avoid at all costs being thought naïve or impulsive, he began to scrutinize the most transparent reports in the interests of his reputation for shrewdness. Whereas, being a big man, he had always bent forward a little to accommodate himself in a friendly way to smaller mortals, he now leaned way over and shambled out of his office with a slightly aggressive lope. This made him known to the public at large as 'The Lion', and to a few mean newspapermen as the 'Missing Link'. At this point my friend could do nothing with him. My friend said, 'A year ago, nothing upset him. He'd go through a report and say – "I think maybe the British ought to look over this page. I don't know anything about the British, but if I'd had a Navy for three or four hundred years, this paragraph would hurt. Better get somebody to tone it down. No sense at this stage pulling rank on the British." ' 'Now,' my friend went on, 'he's timid and he's started to talk gobbledegook.' Gobbledegook was the immortal word given by a famous Texan to government language, or Federal prose, the sort of prose which doesn't say 'I'd like fifty pursuit planes and like 'em fast,' but says 'Personnel will take cognizance of a high priority requisition of fifty pursuit planes. Immediate implementation of this policy directive is imperative.'

The old man stayed on in his job. And the end of it was the awful last stage in the acquisition of a public personality: the trick now was to find ways of doing good work, making lively policy, either without the old man's knowing about it, or by long preliminary massages of his ego to the point where he thought *he* had invented all the best ideas. Well, mercifully, Hitler committed suicide, and the Germans caved in, and they do say we won. The old man was retired, with citations, awards, honorary degrees from universities, and a big testimonial dinner at which he said that Washington had taught him one great and humble thing about our democratic system, that 'if a man who had grown from his roots by the Penniquash River brought to a great office the same qualities he had learned from his neighbours, he had something precious to offer in the service of his country'. There was loud applause, and two newspapermen who had been assigned to cover the old man's department promptly took an overdose of extract of barley and knew no pain for days. The old man went home to the Penniquash River, where he fished again, rediscovered his own friends (while they rediscovered him) and generally practised the painful chore of easing himself back into the shafts. He breaks rein once in a while and sounds off to everybody's boredom at a Chamber of Commerce dinner, or some such, about the perils to the national security of a policy left in the hands of the present government in Washington: that would be, just for the record, the government that gently retired him. Otherwise, he's recovered a lot of his old whimsicality and directness, even if it now has a fruity, mellow tang which has earned him the title of the Elder Statesman of the Penniquash River. They say that he sometimes doesn't know where to hang his coat.

WASHINGTON, D.C.

In the Library of Congress in Washington, in the catacombs devoted to the Fine Arts, there is a wonderful piece of nonsense – a painting done by a British artist with the forthright title, *The Burning of Washington by the British in 1814*. It is a boy's recreation of what was certainly a lurid but also a workmanlike and almost casual piece of destruction. The Americans, who were then in the downy youth of their nationalism, being only twenty-seven years old, had an itch to flex their muscles and get into a fight with the Champ – Great Britain, need I say. They had neither the army, the navy nor the money to fight anybody, and the British regulars landing in Maryland joined up with the British marines stationed in Chesapeake Bay, who broke their snooze, yawned slightly and walked forty miles to Washington. There they calmly burned down the Capitol, the White House – then known as the President's Palace – and the rest of the new public buildings that in those days were all that distinguished Washington from a fishing town on a marsh. It must have been a very humiliating event, for the President and his wife had to lodge in a boarding-house, and Congress was forced to meet in the Post Office, which had (in the general boredom of the undertaking) been overlooked.

Anyway, the British artist who painted this picture made of it the sort of three-colour advertisement that nations conscious of their strength insist on in their official art, the sort of thing which is now reproduced on breakfast-food containers, under some such title as American Victories, First Series. The picture shows the banks of the Potomac River ringed with cannon. Across the river come the British marines, either standing astride small sailboats, or pointing swords with one knee crooked in the approved position of my Lord Nelson, or sitting placidly rowing and admiring the view. And what a view! Nothing seems to be actually burning, because this would rob the spectator of the careful drawing of proud little buildings that are *about* to be burnt. But from every bridge and tower and roof to the horizon puffs what looks like a swarm of barrage balloons, or those wavy circles that enclose the dialogue in comic strips. It is fire and flame. And even the harmless American ships on the opposite shore are writhing in great bags of smoke as impressive as medical illustrations of ulcerated intestines.

The contrast must be obvious between these valiant red-coats waving swords, and the British Treasury experts periodically sitting down in that same city showing their account books to the Americans who can have little fear that the White House will shortly go up in flames. But the contrast I want to go into is not so much about our sadly reversed status as between Washington then and now. Washington exists in everybody's eye as a newsreel image of a dome, a huge statue of Lincoln, a parade of some sort, and Mr Truman on the White House lawn, receiving a model fire-hydrant from the fire chief of Oskawassa, Arkansas. Washington is so much a source and factory of the daily news that we rarely pause in our sleuthing to see what sort of a town it is and who are the people who live there.

Well, it is a town made in the triangular join of two rivers. When I say a town 'made', I mean made. For it is the legitimate boast of Americans that theirs is, like Canberra, one of the few national capitals which was chosen as a plot of naked land and designed as a centre of government and built up brick by brick, instead of – like most other world capitals – having the honour of 'capital' imposed at some late date on a city already mushrooming into importance.

In 1787 the Continental Congress made a nation, made its constitution, and looked around for a place to call its capital. The Southern states almost seceded in a row over the location, and for a time there never seemed to be a possible chance of the choice falling on what its enemies called 'that Indian place in the wilderness'. However, there was a certain dinner-party given by Jefferson, and a few bottles of smooth Madeira persuaded Alexander Hamilton (in exchange for the support of a bill he was sponsoring) to promise to deliver enough Northern votes to clinch the choice of this area on the Potomac, which was cut out of Maryland and Virginia; which General Washington personally inspected and approved of; and which was chosen and called 'the city of Washington in the district of Columbia'. Washington hired a man called L'Enfant to design a federal city. Now L'Enfant was a Frenchman and an eighteenth-century man. He was hipped on the subject of 'vistas' and the idea, which he lovingly copied from Versailles, of having great diagonal avenues cross a gridiron or rectangular network of long streets. The idea was that everywhere the diagonals crossed a vertical and a horizontal street you would have a three-way vista. You could see poachers in all directions. You could put cannon there as a point of tactics. What's more, you'd be able to see the great buildings, when they got built, for miles. It all sounded very elegant and modern. But the real-estate men liked it because it offered an endless series of money-making intersections. This obsessed Frenchman shocked them greatly when he showed up with his plans. For of the six thousand acres set aside for the city, over three thousand were for highways, preposterously wide avenues, anything from a hundred and sixty feet to four hundred feet wide. President Washington stuck by him, and he got his great diagonal avenues. Which is a blessed thing, because it's about all that's recognizable of L'Enfant's plan and still gives to Washington whatever it has of splendour and spaciousness.

The Congress, then, after wandering from Philadelphia to Princeton, to Annapolis, to Trenton and New York, set up shop in Washington in 1800. But the city had a hard time getting itself built, getting lighting and paving and sewers and water. Nobody wanted to finance it. The Congress showed a healthy instinct in the early days, which it has since unhappily suppressed, of wondering why it should put up money to prolong anybody's stay in a mess of shacks on a plain that rises only forty feet above the noxious Potomac. For I should tell you that, from that day to this, Washington lies securely in what the guide-books call an amphitheatre and what you and I call a swamp. And it has a damp, wheezy, Dickensian sort of winter hardly equalled by London, and a steaming tropical summer not surpassed by the basin of the Nile, or those outposts on the Persian gulf where bad vice-consuls are sent to rot.

For half the nineteenth century, L'Enfant's immense avenues were the joke of all visiting Europeans. To get on to them, you left somebody's house and then, like poor Miss Martineau, had to hoist your skirts, climb a stile or two, slush through a bog on to the highway, and cross a field and a sliver of street to get to another human habitation. Along these Versailles avenues that fell like ornamental swords across a rubbish-heap went big-bellied Congressmen in cutaway coats, hunters in coonskin caps, judges lugging their law books with them, acid New England ladies, Indian chiefs (there were the remnants of thirty tribes there when the so-called Father of His Country moved in to take possession). Dickens said in the eighteen-forties that Washington was a place 'of spacious avenues that begin in nothing and lead nowhere; streets a mile long that only want houses, roads, and inhabitants; public buildings that need but a public to be complete'.

The eighteen-forties were a bustling time, what with railways getting to be taken for granted, and the telegraph, and canals being dug everywhere. To the good businessmen who roamed around Washington hoping for industry and finding none, the capital city was a flop. The towns south of the Potomac managed to get all their land given back to Virginia. Georgetown, to the north, wanted to go back to Maryland but never succeeded. But during the Civil War, Washington was the base of the Northern armies, and into it swarmed everybody who had a favour to sell, a bridge to mend, a new kind of gun, any sort of influence which might help or threaten the Union. It was in those years, and in the lush and corrupt days of the Reconstruction, that Washington became what it has ever since remained – the headquarters not only of the government but also of pressure groups and lobbyists, of manufacturers and pimps and fixers who conceived of a capital as a city dedicated to the manufacture of wealth by intimidating the government. The District itself was in wretched need of money. Its citizens were Americans without a vote (they still are) or a city government to call their own.

It had a debt of about four million dollars, which in 1874 was increased to twenty-two million. The Federal Government had to guarantee this debt and it wasn't paid off until 1922.

In the late seventies it was decided that somebody would have to try and govern the city, and a municipal corporation was formed with three commissioners chosen by the President.

In this period there was a man called Shepherd, a builder, who gave to Washington its second blessing: a wealth of fine trees. He also got the city clean water and workable sewers, but most of all he started planting trees at a furious rate against a howl of protest from people who thought it was a shameless way to waste public money. He lined L'Enfant's great avenues with English elms, thus for ever defeating the original idea of long, uninterrupted vistas. But he made of a marsh the most shady and leafy town in the United States. Today the streets and squares tower with American elms, with sycamores, with all the glorious variety of American oaks, with lindens and willows, with trees from all over the Union and from many foreign places. The little square right opposite the White House, for instance, has a hundred varieties, with spruce, redwood, magnolia, cherry, holly, basswood, and I don't know what else. And springing up in the unlikeliest places is the Oriental gingko, the Chinese pagoda, and ringing the tidal basin those embarrassing Japanese cherry trees, which when we were at war with Japan had to be called something else, but are always the same, and always perfect.

The best guide-books seem to be incapable of describing the physical look of Washington from any place but the air. That may be because the commanding avenues seen from the earth look like deserted parade-grounds. From the air, of course, they look like landing-strips, a misconception that several pilots from the hinterland acted on, until the city built a few years ago a big modern airport well outside the town. The man from Mars might well assume that Washington was, indeed, another name for Athens taken over by the American Air Force. For arising at majestic intervals from great avenues

71

are what to the pilot look like more Greek wedding-cakes than you'd see at a French chef's golden wedding. When you get nearer to those sleek forbidding piles of white stone, cement and plaster of Paris, you might think them more Roman than Greek, and some more vaguely Italian. I doubt, however, whether you could see in Athens or in Rome such an imposing stack of porticos and rows of Ionic columns and saucer-domes and inset-arches. They are, you would be right in guessing, government buildings – the Capitol, the Supreme Court Building, the Treasury – which is almost an Acropolis in itself. Washington started to build in the seventeen-nineties in the inrushing fashion of the Greek revival (a style in which Americans did delicate and beautiful things when they domesticated it in wood, in the South and New England, as the proper frame for houses and little churches). But whatever was good about the earliest Washington buildings is now to be seen only in the White House and the noble Federal houses of Georgetown. For the Greek revival style was soon succeeded by others, by red-brick Georgian of a humble kind, then by Romanesque, then by all the monstrous colonnades and curlycues of the mid-nineteenth century. At the end of that century there was a World's Fair in Chicago, showing the grandiose plaster-of-Paris façades of the Beaux-Arts exhibition in Paris. Ever since then Washington has lusted after these Roman monsters like a Girl Guide after Mark Antony. Washington would be about as intimate as Nuremberg used to be, if this was all. But happily it has a magnificent park, the finest scenery inside a city's environs, said Lord Bryce, of any city he knew. And it crawls through this graveyard like Virginia creeper over a tombstone. The city is also nibbled at on all sides by suburbs – which city isn't? Some of them are old red-brick Georgian and some we'd better just say are suburban. Indeed, if you went to live in Washington and by some strength of character managed not to be a government employee, you might live in many parts of town and say that rows of nineteenth-century boarding-houses were more typical of Washington than rows of Greek columns. It's true; the two shapes most characteristic of Washington are the Italian palace, where the wage-slaves work, and the bow-windows, where they live.

You'll see that it's impossible to talk about Washington without getting preoccupied with the government and its buildings. But that's because there's practically nothing else. Washington is not a capital like London, which is a government capital but also a capital of banking, of music, of theatre, of eating, of writing and reading, of public sports, of shipping. All those things other than government are centred in New York, which Washingtonians contemptuously think of as Babylon-on-the-Hudson. Washington has no permanent theatres – it is wary of opening them to Negroes, and Washington is embarrassed by Negroes for exactly the same reason that Alabama is: nearly a third of its population is coloured.

Washington has little music that can begin to compare with the great orchestras of New York, Boston, Minneapolis, San Francisco or even Philadelphia. It has indifferent public food. It is as close as Baltimore to the huge Chesapeake Bay, but whereas the tables of Baltimore swill with terrapin stew and snapper-turtle soup and groan with expiring lobsters of a fatness that has to be seen to be believed, Washington for some reason makes no decent use of the gorgeous fish that come gasping up at the end of its streets. The answer may be that Washington stays home. It is not a night-owl town. The Congressmen don't like to be seen in their cups in public. And I doubt if either Sodom or Gomorrah was ever kept going by a population of respectable clerks.

This is another – in fact, the major – by-product of Washington's being nothing but a government city. It is the only town I know which has bred its own species of employee – the 126 clerks who came here in 1800 were neat and sober and have neatly and soberly reproduced their kind, to the tune of 300,000 government clerks. You do not see here the clashing variety of human shape and style and colouring that makes American cities such a challenge to the pleasant senses and some others. In other national capitals it is on the streets that you see mankind's variety. It is indoors – inside the courts and the parliament – that you see a mass of officials, who look as if they'd been run off on an assembly line. Not so in Washington. Here all the types in America, and all the accents, are drawn from the plains and mountains and deserts into the House and Senate Chambers. And on the streets – a population of quiet, slim, self-effacing people in glasses. Indoors, the human jungle, outdoors – the clerks. For it is the Congress and its hangers-on that ride the roost and set the tone of high life. You do not walk down the Strand side-stepping M.P.s at every turn or cluster around a church to catch Mr Aneurin Bevan at his devotions. In London the Members of Parliament enjoy their true glory only when they are inside the House of Commons. Once outside they dissolve into the formidable and dominant race known as the Cockneys. But in Washington the politicians, the puffing *gauleiters* from the provinces, are the rulers. It is this status which gives to the natives of Washington a meek subterranean life, like that of Parisians during the occupation. They are resigned to it, as a Blackpool landlady is resigned to the profitable uproar of August Bank Holiday.

So, to continue what Mr Churchill would call 'this true account', we have a government capital obsessed and absorbed with governing, and all the feuds and deals and crises that go with it. We have a city with poor food, a nightmare of a climate, dignified by great avenues and by the cascading foliage of magnificent trees. But how, you must be saying, how about the high life, the air of great events, the intrigue?

It is usual to say that Washington is a nest of intrigue. And so it is. And undoubtedly there are more luxurious and louder parties held there than most of the ancient capitals can any longer afford. In this country you would expect the social arbiter to be a woman. And so she is. But ever since Mrs Perle Mesta got made the Minister to Luxembourg there has been a fine rivalry going on, and much well-bred meowing in well-kept gardens, about who is to succeed Mrs Mesta as the town's leading hostess. I should add here that though not many Washington wives can aspire to toss a battalion of pressed duck at a thousand guests, Washington wives are another breed all to themselves. I never yet met a wife of a man anywhere near the government who didn't bear up splendidly under the intimate knowledge that her husband really swung the election

74

and gave the word for the date of the invasion of Europe. This all, surely, implies a very harem of intrigue.

But intrigue in a capital city suggests the splendid briberies of a Talleyrand, the sort of masked ball at which the Secretary of State forgets to dance with the wife of the Turkish ambassador and boom! – another Crusade is on the march. Washington is indeed choking with intrigue and gossip. But its intrigue is less like that of the court of Louis XIV and more like that of a vast church bazaar, in which hot-eyed matrons wink and whisper in the hope that Mrs X's pickles will be rejected as too tart and Farmer Y's Poland Farceurs will come in a poor third.

You have heard the word 'pork-barrel' – the President's pork-barrel – and must have wondered what a pork-barrel was doing in so elegant a place as the White House. It is, alas, a permanent though invisible fixture. To be more accurate, it is two fixtures. For there's one pork-barrel for the President and one for the Congress. Like many another American institution, they were created by self-denial and ended by giving a licence to self-indulgence.

Jefferson and his excellent Secretary of the Treasury followed the English custom of using the national income as they thought fit, disbursing lump sums to each department and accounting for the money when the money was spent. But at the first complaint from Congress they decided to adopt the more chivalrous method of asking the Congress to specify its wants and name a price for each of them. The result is the Congressional pork-barrel, which persuades some Congressmen to postpone forever their interest in what is best for the nation and sends them circulating through back-rooms, offices and parties, ogling an old friend here and charming a stranger there, in the hope of swiping for their constituency an army camp, or getting a new post office built or an old river drained.

The President's private pork-barrel was left him by the Constitution as a consolation prize for having to get the Senate's consent to his appointment of all the big Federal jobs, like Cabinet officers and ambassadors. He was allowed to keep certain 'inferior offices', which his party has ever since been eager to help him fill. He it is who appoints a postmaster in Santa Claus, Arizona, a food inspector in New Orleans, a tax collector in Red Cent, Utah. If this seems a harmless vanity, it should be remembered that there are many thousands of these 'inferior offices' scattered across the land and that every one of them represents a Congressman appeased or a Congressman flouted. They tot up to a nice balance of favours and insults that registers with painful accuracy when some bill the President is dying to have passed comes to the vote in the Congress. On a dark day of the Civil War, Lincoln confessed he looked more ashen than usual not from any concern about his armies but because he was worried over a postmastership in Brownsville, Ohio.

Washington was accordingly long ago described as 'a huge hog-wallow where every man's snout is at the pork-barrel'. It is an uncouth image, no doubt, but it is a truer symbol of Washington intrigue than any boudoir gallivanting ever recorded in the White House. Washington tries to perfume this reality with a lot of scented legend about George Washington's eye for a pretty ankle, and how Martha Washington was a fragrant thing in her day. But even this myth doesn't hold up. In our day she has given her name to a wholesome candy. Imagine 'Josephine Buonaparte Cough Drops'!

You have seen that I have done my best to give you a vivid and unprejudiced account of this great capital city where now the ancient empires bow to the dollar. I should like to take you around some more of its glories, but, like Mr Fitzpatrick in the travelogues, we must say a reluctant farewell to the federal city on the Potomac. And so as the sun sinks into the Tidal Basin ... excuse me, I have just time to make the fast train up to Babylon-on-the-Hudson.

NEW YORK, NEW YORK

An English novelist came through New York a little time ago and, as all travellers must, brooded awhile about our ways. When he got home he did a radio talk about it. Nothing more would have been heard about it if the script of this talk had not been reprinted in *The New York Times*. It was no sooner out than the ambulances were summoned to handle a rush of high-blood-pressure cases, and the mail-trucks dumped bags of protests on *The New York Times*. From these outcries you would never have guessed that Mr Priestley had just been a delegate to the United Nations Educational, Scientific and Cultural Organization, and that he was a man chosen to spread light and understanding among us.

Too bad, said Mr Priestley, that New York's skyscrapers are not dedicated 'to God or to some noble aspect of communal life' but only to 'buying and selling dividends'. 'Is that so?' asked one correspondent. 'Then let me tell him that the American Bible Society, the American Association of Social Workers, the American Cancer Society, the Medical Society of New York and the British Information Services, to name only a few', don't buy and sell dividends. Mr Rockefeller of course might plead guilty, but his conviction would carry the reminder that his skill in these things helped to cure a lot of dysentery and scurvy in tropical places and helped a lot of Englishmen to come to the United States and have the leisure, after their work with microscopes, to share some of Mr Priestley's feelings about New York. Mr Priestley conceded that this was 'just a passing thought'.

'It seems hardly worth while holding on to,' snapped this New Yorker.

As for the dismal state of the drama in these parts our man referred Mr Priestley to the theatre pages of the newspapers, 'where he will note many plays he may later see in London'.

New York is overcrowded, complained Mr Priestley. Granted, said the New Yorker, but New York takes to people and likes to crowd them in.

I creep into the argument at this point only because I possess a rather dog-eared but still unexpired credential. It is that I have lived in New York steadily – continuously, anyway – for nearly fifteen years; that I came here first as a transatlantic visitor, on money dished out from one of Mr Harkness's sky-scrapers; and that in those days I saw New York much as Mr Priestley sees it now. I think we were both wrong. And I hope it will throw light on more places than New York if I try to say why.

Neither a native nor a traveller can ever be objective about any place on the map. And all we can sensibly discuss is how true for each of them are their feelings about the place. There is a special flow of moods in a traveller. And I think Mr Priestley now, and I nineteen years ago, were talking more about ourselves than about New York. Because travellers are never the same at home and abroad. They always think they are, but the people you travel among notice pretty soon that you have thrown off your responsibilities to your own country and don't have to take on any of theirs. This is the state of natural anarchy and for some grown-ups is the only time they know again the huge relief of kids when school's out. Travellers, however, once they are no longer young and scampy, feel embarrassed, not to say guilty, about their free-dom. They can express it in one of two ways. They can be secretly frightened by the alien life around them and retreat more tenaciously than ever into habits that belong to their country and nowhere else. Hence the cricket clubs in Brazil and Hollywood, which, I have noticed, manage to recruit some Britons who would not be playing cricket at home. I have known Englishmen who in England can take their tea or leave it but who get to insist on it in the United States, pre-cisely because afternoon tea is not a custom of the country.

The other reflex looks like the opposite, but deep in the springs of our childish fear it may be only another reaction to the same threat. It is to go out and do with much bravery all the things you do not do at home. Thus the Englishman who becomes a baseball fan or learns to shudder at Brussels sprouts. This is a plucky show that he is no longer bound by nostalgia or habit to the old life he left behind him.

I believe there is a peculiar mythical appeal to Englishmen in the distant prospect of America. It may go as far back as the Elizabethans, the travellers' tales of fat turkeys, gigantic oysters and succulent fruits, the news of an Eldorado begging for settlement. 'Oh my America, my new founde land!' cried Donne, though at that particular moment he wasn't thinking of leaving home. This myth has been modified down the years, until there are at least two or three generations of Britons conditioned by a whole childhood literature about the West, and now by the glittering stereotypes of the movies, and more regrettably by the solid tradition of reporting back to England only what is corrupt or eccentric or scandalous. From this there emerges a modern myth about America, some of which is poetic and true, some of which is a punching-bag for stay-at-homes. The city of New York has come to crystallize the nightmare aspect of this dream country. It becomes a hard and hideous place, with frightening canyons of skyscrapers. Its life is, in Mr Priestley's words, 'restless ... in its nightly pursuit of diminishing pleasures. Not a flower,' he moans, 'can blossom on these concrete cliffs.' Well, I am told that in the granite veins of this city, on Manhattan alone, they have found a hundred and seventy varieties of semi-precious stones. Slit into this grey hunk of rock we inhabit there are garnets and amethysts and opals and beryls and tourmalines, and other jewels even less pronounceable. There are still about half as many trees as human beings. And the commonest backyard tree is the ailanthus, which – I hate to tell Mr Priestley – the Chinese call the tree of heaven.

But this doesn't fit in with anything Europeans have been told, and the heck with it. To more Europeans than would admit it, there is always at the back of the mind this neon-lit image of New York as Babylon, where innocence is banished, where anything goes, where everything has its price, where – in the vivacious version current among my schoolmates in England – you rode a perpetual shoot-the-chutes and bounded the waves of pleasure, to the music of Duke Ellington, while at your side snuggled a beautiful girl, beautiful and up to no good.

If you think I am romancing about this, let me remind you that the symbol of an island of pleasure, presided over by a beckoning female, is almost a constant of the human imagination. It was Circe in Greece, Izanami in Japan, Semiramis who built Babylon. These, you may say, are only legends. But what is more real and indispensable than the ideas that burst into life from men's imaginations precisely because they do not exist? They express the permanent dissatisfactions of man with his lot, and this particular one relieves the secret fear that, like Marley's ghost, we may be wasting our days on earth weaving chains of bankbooks, files, ledgers, insurance policies.

When Mr Priestley calls New York 'Babylon piled on Imperial Rome', I think he is the victim of this myth. Once you stay and live in this city, you have to admit that it is nothing of the sort. The intelligentsia will claim that New York tries to be the city they would like to despise. But the intelligentsia is the same everywhere and is a poor guide to the real life of cities. And to the people who live this life, the overpowering number of middle-class New Yorkers, who have as much town pride as Leeds or Manchester, there was one sentence of old Jeremiah Priestley's that really hurt: 'The lonely heart of man cannot come home here.'

No? On Manhattan Island alone (and Mr Priestley was talking about only one of the five boroughs) there are two million people who won't live anywhere else and wouldn't want to, even after three drinks. New York is their home town. It is not Babylon. It is the place where we rise in the mornings to the clicking of the radiator or the bawling of the downstairs brat. We take in the milk. We descend on the schools with a rush of kisses and a greeting of neighbours. We head for the subway. We hear a great bass reverberate over the island. It is not, as Mr Priestley might suspect, the trump of doom. It is only the *basso profundo* of the *Queen Elizabeth* going downriver. We spend the day at work, restlessly perhaps to the extent of leaving home for a distant workshop and then at the end of the day reversing the process and leaving the workshop to get home again. Maybe, if it is not slushy or damp, we decide to walk home and watch a copper sun sinking into an El Greco sky over against the Jersey shore. If the skies of New York often lift us, miserable ants that we are, into delusions of grandeur, we will often spot on the corner, as we turn to go in our building, something casual or scurrilous that restores us to the affectionate human scale. On the wall of a bricked-up lot a tiny New Yorker scribbled a typical sentence. 'Nuts,' it said. 'Nuts to all the boys on Second Avenue' – a long struggling pause, then the concession, 'except between 68th and 69th Streets.'

We come in and we play with the children or bawl them out. We enjoy, if we have any sense, the variety of the people of our town, and there is often some crazy thing to tell. I have daily dealings with a score of Americans whom I shall only identify here as an Italian shoeshine man, a garrulous German elevator man, a warm, wisecracking Jewish news-agent, and a range of shopkeepers who span the gamut of New York names from Mr O'Byrne De Witt to Circumstance H. Smith, a Negro with fine manners.

The thermometer dips overnight and we look forward to tomorrow, when the red ball goes up over Central Park – no signal for revolution this, Mr Priestley, or even retribution, but the City's cue to tell us there's going to be skating. Whenever we go to the Park and find, say, there's not enough sand in the sand box the children play in, we telephone the office of Mr Moses, the Park Commissioner. Next morning two attendants come along with replenishing boxes of sand. The city works pretty hard on the organizing of the citizen's play, and in summer there are handball courts to be repaired, there are city band concerts, city outdoor opera, city fish to be fed into the surrounding streams, and swimming for thousands who leap the trains for the vast city-sponsored lay-out of Jones Beach.

In the evening, what do we do? Well, I see from a city survey that only one in fifteen of us has ever been in a night-club. We sit and read, or have friends in, listen to the radio or go to lectures, or a movie, play pinochle or checkers or poker, putter with this and that. And ninety-two in a hundred of us begin to go to bed around ten-thirty.

81

Our days and months are bound by work, and fun, and quarrels, and taxes, and movies and savings, and children and death and friendship. When we are far from home we think of New York, and it is not of Circe with a henna rinse bawling into a night-club microphone. We see in imagination the white steam hissing through the pavements. We smell the fishy smell of the Fulton market, or the whiff of chicory over Foley Square, or the malty brew that hangs around the East Nineties. We recall the Bronx Zoo, and Mercury standing on his muscular thighs over the traffic lights on Fifth Avenue. We see in the mind's eye the magic dioramas of Africa and Hawaii in the Museum of Natural History, or the pink front page of the morning tabloids. We hear of a girl who was loaded with furs and automobiles by a sharpie using absconded funds. Over the transatlantic wires they flash her confession: 'I never knew he was in an illegal business. He told me he was a gambler.' Glory be! We know her for our own.

Or some dank day in Brittany or Paris, we recall the one day in three or four that is blindingly clear, brilliant as a knight in armour, the sun slashing down the avenues like a sword. On such a day, my cab-driver stopped for a red light at St Patrick's. And so did a herd of young teenagers before they turned in to say their prayers. Most of them, I should say, were in sweaters of every colour. He leered at their faces and caught their twinkling shapes in the shafts of sunlight. He hit the steering-wheel with his open hand. And said to me, or perhaps to God: 'They come in all shapes and sizes. Yes, sir. Great stuff. Whaddya say, Mac?' He laughed himself silly.

Restless we *are*, and very small, threading through our canyons. But are we, as Mr Priestley assures us we are, 'full of unease, disquiet, bewilderment'? Last summer Dr Gallup found that over ninety per cent of us thought we were happy. Suppose we allow ten per cent for pride or bravado and another ten per cent for Mr Priestley's transatlantic insight. That still leaves seventy per cent who believe, maybe wrongly, that they are happy. Better let 'em wallow in their ignorance, Mr Priestley, these placid dopes who don't even know when they're 'deeply bewildered and frustrated'. Whaddya say, Mac?

THE SEASONS

WINTER – AND FLORIDA

There is a British delusion that you have to go South or West in America to see anything resembling a beautiful landscape. The North-east and the Midwest, these travellers say, are a dull and poverty-stricken thing. This is not a prejudice, for it is an observation made on the spot. But the reason it is so often made must be because most Englishmen who contrive to come here at all – on something called 'business' – do so usually in winter. And it must be said that there is surely no landscape known to temperate man that is so shorn and blighted by the coming on of winter.

Most of New England is glacial country and is, geologically speaking, a rocky shambles made by an ice-sheet that ground its massive way eastwards, ripped off the tops of hills and scattered a hailstorm of stones and boulders in all the lowlands. It also smeared some places with layers of good soil. But the only crop you can absolutely depend on anywhere through New England and along the North Atlantic coastal plain is a crop of stones. So, although New England is God's garden to a native (unless he happens to be a farmer), to an Englishman it is pretty rough ground. I remember one Briton who lived here moodily for years until he found the source of his homesickness: 'There isn't a field you can lie down in,' he said. This may sound very fussy but when you consider that the grass-pack of the pasture regions of Iowa and Minnesota is the pride of the United States, and that it is still only about one-third as tight and luscious as the grass-pack of southern England, it is easy to see why southern Englishmen can seem so snooty when real-estate men confront them with a 'rural paradise' in Connecticut.

The North Atlantic coastal plain suffers in the same way from having had its face ground down by that old continental ice-sheet. Then it has been bruised by industry. This all sounds very forlorn. But there is enough forest still to smother and glorify the land from spring through the autumn. Then we run into our regular blight – a winter keen and cold that blasts the land and withers it. And it is from mid-November on through March that we can appreciate, if we weren't born here, the remark of a Californian who said that if the United States had been settled from the Pacific Coast eastwards, New England would still be undiscovered.

From the Atlantic to the Rockies then, at this time of the year, the winds whistle and the snows descend. And in the North-east the boulders stare at the sky, the stubbly grass turns brown and skimpy, the trees go naked as seedling tele-graph poles. Towns and villages that are dense with green when the foliage crowns them are stripped down to hard, brown earth and collections of box-like houses and shacks dropped as aimlessly as the boulders.

By mid-November the ordinary inhabitant of the North Atlantic coast lives on a lifeless slab of rock and soil. I say 'ordinary inhabitant' because there have been American naturalists from Thoreau to John Kieran who make a virtue of this bleak necessity and go peering for microscopic flowers and lizards beneath the stones. They reverse the doubtful com-pliment Robert Benchley once paid the British: 'It is not that the British take their pleasures sadly but that they take pleasure in such tiny, tiny things.'

To most of us, though, who know a tree as something with leaves, the winter is a thing to be endured. True, we have lots of sunshine and there is an exhilaration in the sharp light and the crunching snows. But come November, and again in February and March, we wish we were somewhere else. We get up in the morning and stumble over to the window and look at the thermometer on the outside to know what to wear when we get outside. I realize, if I recall my European homes correctly, that it is an American's privilege to wake in the morning and slosh around naked without knowing what the weather's like outside. But comfort, like cocaine, demands an increasing dosage. And by December it is not enough to be warm indoors and cold out. It would be nice to be warm all the time. So for Americans with money saved, no matter what their kind or class ('income group' as we airily say) December is the month that suggests one beckoning word – Florida. It is the time when the rich, the comfortably idle, the alimony-plated divorcée, the Midwest farmer with his crops in, the tired performers in a circus troupe, the business executive with a couple of weeks' holiday in hand, the exceptional showgirl bored with the nightly routine on Broadway, the well-heeled black marketeer, the leisured grandmother and the grandchildren she dotes on, the cab-driver about to switch employers, the gangster and the race-track tout – all of them abed at night dream the same dream and see themselves lying in not much more than a coat of golden tan on a gypsum beach, the sand fine as sugar, the lapping sea of a shining aquamarine. You will detect a slight sneer in the tone of this account of the people who are off to Florida, and I hope you will interpret it correctly as nothing more than envy.

Ponce de Leon, the first white man to touch the Florida coast, in 1513, thought he would find there the fountain of youth. And De Soto, twenty-six years later, went looking for gold. Four hundred years later, in a nation which clings to its youth more than any nation, the day-dream of the winter visitor is much the same. And the centuries shake hands in the spectacle of an ageing Midwestern farmer and his wife driving south-east in a De Soto car, or a showgirl off on the night train for Miami and a little private project of her own, from which digging for gold is not excluded.

It would depress a Floridian to hear me approach his state in this, the condescending northern, way. For to most Americans Florida is not a state but a state of mind, not a place to live at all but a place to work off a year's inhibitions in a few determined weeks of pleasure. But Florida itself is a little to blame for this reputation. Though it has a great trade in citrus fruit, and a developing cattle-market, a cigar industry and a wealth of what Americans call folk-ways, it boasts that its most marketable commodity is its climate. And it spends millions of dollars a year describing that climate in print in the hope of attracting, and attracting back, into the state several score million dollars' worth of winter tourists. As early as 1910 a newspaper in St Petersburg, on the west coast of the peninsula, offered to give away its whole daily edition any time in the year when the sun failed to shine before three in the afternoon. They have had to pay the forfeit no more than four or five times a year.

Before going into the life of a state that has been called the last economic frontier, and which I should call the Unknown State, it might be as well to picture where it is and what it looks like.

It hangs down from the extreme eastern corner of the United States like a pistol held at the head of the Caribbean. The handle touches Alabama. The chamber forms the coast that faces on the Gulf of Mexico. The long barrel pointing south and west forms the peninsula, four hundred miles long, and it is this that means Florida to Americans. What they *think* of, however, as Florida is the shining rim of the pistol's foresight – the linked strands of beaches where in the past twenty years towering hotels, shops in rainbow colours, yacht harbours, trailer* camps, and a whole market-place of pleasure has been built on a long strip of coastline literally dredged up from the ocean. There was a time only a generation ago when no one probed this ocean except Greek sponge-fishers, who have now settled westward along the Gulf Coast. But today the ocean dashes gently against the most expensive bodies, the best-fed stomachs, and some of the sharpest heads in America. Today the offshore waters flash with dinghies and yachts from which, as Westbrook Pegler says, 'fishermen use little fish the size of billygoats as bait for fish the size of cows'.

Like many another American institution, then, Florida is the victim of its advertising. Of course, the curse of bad advertising is that it creates a false issue which the wise as well as the stupid come to think is the essential thing to talk about; so that even people who repudiate the advertising don't know anything else to look for. If they don't like salt water or find the beach-life vacuous, then that is all there is to Florida, and it's a miserable thing.

The physical approach to the pleasure domes of Miami and Miami Beach contributes to this deception. For it is not what the travel-folders illustrate. You cross the Georgia border and streak monotonously over bare, cut-over pineland. You may

* Caravan.

just glimpse a few Negroes chipping the pine trees for gum, which is then distilled into turpentine. But mostly you will see nothing but sandy wastes, decorated at times by piles of lumber. A few cattle, and pigs snuffling in cypress swamps. You race through run-down shrimp ports. Slowly the vegetation, such as there is of it, gets more tropical, but never lush. Cabbage palms blob by, and at the water's edge you see cormorants trundling, like model planes in trouble. The last hundred miles are an assault and battery by advertising. Haphazard battalions of billboards go by, advertising miraculously profitable orange groves, night-clubs, trailer camps, ice cream, real estate ('This is God's country – you'd be at home in Heaven'). Your mileage is calculated for you by roadside signs screaming – 'Only ten miles to tupelo honey', or two miles to an alligator farm, or 'Twelve miles to Sandy's super-duper jumbo hamburgers'. Occasionally there is a crude sign painted by some wandering evangelist and striking a chillier note: 'Prepare to Meet Thy God'.

You might remember that sign when you come to open the state guidebook and find on an early page this warning: 'Caution to Tourists: do not enter bushes at the sides of highway; snakes and redbugs usually infest such places'. That may be a shock to the tourist, but if he followed it up he might go on to learn something of the state as it is only ten miles inland from Miami's garish suburbs, and there meet a Florida that is much as it was a thousand years ago. In none of the forty-eight states does life leap so suddenly, in an hour's motor drive, from the suburban snooze to the primeval ooze. Only a thin strip of pine and palmetto woods stands guardian between what we laughingly call 'civilization as we know it' and the seething cypress swamp known as the Everglades; where four hundred species and sub-species of birds carol and whine over a slimy wilderness dignified by the white plumes of the egret; where orchid trees of a thousand blooms rise out of the pure muck that seems to have inundated the whole visible earth. It is at night that this contrast is most compelling. And you feel it most dramatically going west from Miami. Go by plane and in a minute or two Miami is a scum of bright bubbles on the edge of a stagnant pond. Or drive out at twilight, as the floodlights are switched on to the vertical hotels, and the bartenders begin to rattle their ice, and blondes with coal-black tans appear in their backless finery. Within a half-hour Miami is a memory of a Hollywood musical to a man stranded on the Amazon. An eagle circles against a purple sky. A buzzard flaps away from some dark carrion on the road ahead. You stop your motor and see no living thing. But the loneliness, and the awe of living close to a jungle before it was ever tamed into lumber or tailored into farms or gardens, is intensified by the insane symphony of sound that strikes your ear. Over a bubbling, rumbling percussion of bullfrogs, you will hear the chuck-chuck of tropical woodpeckers, the wheezy sigh of bull-rats, a low slush of crocodile. If you are lucky you may see the scarlet glowing wing of a flamingo. The din lets up for a moment, and then you are terrified into alertness again by a thin wailing sound, like that of a lost man gone crazed. It is the everyday song of a water-bird that hobbles as it walks and is known as the limpkin.

Yet inside this dense inland swamp there are living humans who seldom come out. They are the Seminole Indians, who have mingled with the white man possibly less than any other tribe in the United States. They have a long and resentful history of relations with him and there is no certainty that they yet regard themselves as being at peace with the United States government. A final treaty of peace between the Seminoles and the government was signed in 1934, and another 'final' treaty in 1937. They live entirely by hunting and they hunt well. Because most of the land is under water, they live on encampments built of dried tree-trunks fastened together like the spokes of a wheel. The family pots and pans are anchored nearby on rafts. When it's wet they sleep on platforms made of saplings above the swamp and covered with a roof of palm leaves. Here, one hour from Miami, they worship their god Yo-He-Wah, who is the symbol of all virtue and purity and love, and whose name may never be mentioned except at a religious festival. They disapprove of capital punishment, they rule themselves with a council of medicine men, and they have rather curious beliefs about marriage. Being so near and yet so far from the civilized whites of Miami and Palm Beach, they look on marriage as a sacred and serious undertaking which may only be severed – indeed must be severed – for a single reason. The reason is 'incompatibility'. There are no other grounds for divorce, because in their primitive way they think it is a crime to stay married to someone you no longer love.

This contrast between the pleasure industry of Miami and the timeless life of the Seminoles, between a façade of civilization and the primitive culture that lies behind it, is not unique in the United States. You might recall the community of Salt Lake City and the almost unexplored Robber's Roost country that lies not far away. The luxury hotels and saloons of Las Vegas, Nevada, lie on the very edge of the fearful Mojave desert. You might even discover that only ninety miles from New York is the fashionable resort of Southampton and scratching its handsome back is the scrubby reservation of the Shinnecock Indians. But nowhere is the contrast so extreme as it is in Florida. It is so vivid to the tourist that he comes into Florida and goes out of it under the impression that the state has nothing behind the night-clubs, the beaches and the race-track but a mess of swamp. However, when the tourists depart in the late winter, they leave behind one half the winter population. These are the two million Floridians who live neither on the east coast nor in the swamp. They have a life of their own, and it is time to talk about them, who inhabit the other three-quarters of the Unknown State.

Running down the centre of the peninsula and across to its west coast is a lakeland district, which is busy harvesting Florida's second money crop – the first being, of course, the tourists. These people, too, sell the climate, in the shape of oranges and grapefruit and, since the war, in the shape of little tins containing their concentrated juices. The government set up a laboratory early in the war to make citrus concentrate under the Lend-Lease programme. It was a brilliant reply to the challenge of the Nazi submarines, which just then were sinking Allied tankers and freighters every night from the Jersey Coast to the Florida keys. One ship-load of concentrate could be converted when it was safe in port into as much orange-juice as it would otherwise take five ships to carry. The conversion process is very simple. It requires one housewife and running water.* Each tin of concentrate can be watered down to make whole orange-juice of five times the volume of the original. Like other expedients thought up in wartime, this experiment done in the name of the Allies is now paying off handsomely for the natives. For the government, in its little laboratory at Dunedin, incidentally disposed of a prejudice that is common not only to you and me but to the Florida orange-growers. It is the idea that oranges are something to get juice out of. The firm that took over and expanded the government laboratory when the war was over is now a very profitable commercial enterprise canning a fortune in concentrated orange-juice and boasting that orange-juice is a by-product. Once the juice is out, they are left with what used to be thrown away: with the pulp, the peel, the seeds. Now they extract from the seeds oleomargarine, vegetable fats for cooking, and a dye that will fix any known colour in artificial silk. From the coloured layer of the peel they extract terpenes for battleship paint, and carotene, which provides trillions of units a year of vitamin A. From the white pulp they get pectin, a superlative jelling agent and a medical godsend for the early treatment of deep wounds. That still leaves cellulose and sugar, from which they take ethyl alcohol for gun cotton, the vitamin B complex, and feed yeast for cattle. So the orange grove has turned into a chemical industry.

They joke in Florida about how, at the end of the winter, a trainload of millionaires going home will be shunted on to a siding to let a trainload of cabbages go through. If you are a Florida truck-farmer (a market gardener, as you'd say) this is no joke. Most of the land of Florida is poor land, and of its thirty-five million acres only two million are in crops. The climate of the central region and the Gulf Coast is not much more genial than the climate of Georgia and South Carolina to the north. So in late winter there's always a race on to ship north the vegetables which in a few weeks will be ready for delivery from Georgia and the Carolinas. They will be harvesting them up there in the early spring, and once they start that is the end of the Florida crop. Hence when a train of

* The same hazard of war, and the identical ingenuity, were responsible in the sixteenth century for the invention of brandy.

cabbages starts north, the signals go down all the way and there's nobody important enough to slow it, especially if the weather in the Carolinas has taken a turn for the better.

Floridians have always regretted having to wince when anybody mentions beef or praises the cattle bred in Texas and fattened in Kansas and Iowa. Florida has been trying for a hundred years to build up a cattle-bowl to compete with Texas. But scrub pineland is not the best pasture. And Florida was pestered for decades by a tick which other states killed off through compulsory cattle-dipping laws. The Florida cattle-men would not dip their cattle, and when the state tried to make them they dynamited the vats. They were rebellious be-cause they knew that the Florida tick is a special bug that thrives not only on cattle but on deer and dogs and horses. You can imagine the feelings of the race-track owners when a quarantine was extended to racehorses. But there was no hope for a cattle industry until the cattlemen gave in. Just before the war they submitted and today, if you drive through central Florida, you will see the surest sign of ambitious cattle-raising: forest fires blazing everywhere – the favourite method, and in this poor land the compulsory method, of burning the range for better pasture.

You may have been trying to picture the people of Florida. It is quite a strain. For Florida is in the South but not of it. Two-party politics rears its hydra head again. Most of the native Southerners are in the north of the state; the southern part is ninety per cent northern, people who came here in the last forty years to retire, to run a small orange farm, to sell real estate, to mock at their families stuck in the northern winters. But there are two industries run by what you can be bold enough to call traditional Floridians, by people who are not seen on beaches, who seldom pitch horseshoes and never lunch at tables carrying a vase of camellias.

They are the cigar industry and the turpentine industry. The cigar industry offers an ironic little essay in labour relations. Eighty years ago some Cuban cigar-makers came up to Key West to avoid the import duty on Cuban cigars and to free themselves from the pressure of a growing Cuban labour union. But the cigar-workers promptly started their unions in

Key West. Mr Ybor, the leading manufacturer, who must have heard about the boundless possibilities of self-expression in God's country, decided to move his pitch. He moved his factories once more. But the unions didn't have to move. They just growed wherever the manufacturer moved his tent. Mr Ybor eventually landed up in Tampa. There were only a few hundred people there in 1880. Today there are about fifteen thousand Cubans, nine thousand Spaniards and nine thousand Italians. Every kind of 'discipline' was exercised to suppress the growing unions and in the nineteen-twenties there was a militant parade of the Ku Klux Klan. But, one cigar-worker recalled, 'We just sat on our porches with our guns across our laps and watched the parade. It sure was a quiet parade.' The strike that brought on this visitation of the familiar hooded men lasted ten months and the Florida cigar-trade has never regained what it lost to its competitors. In 1935 the older cigar-workers sent a petition to the Cuban Government asking to be taken back and pensioned off. Nothing came of it. The travel literature tells you of the glow and charm of the Latin life of the cigar-workers. Perhaps they are thinking of a coloured witch-doctor, just out of jail for practising voodoo, who sneaks from shack to wretched shack in Tampa selling charms to wear around the neck, a particular high-priced charm guaranteed 'to ward off unemployment'.

The turpentine industry, the chipping of pine trees for the resinous gum, which is then distilled to get turpentine and rosin, is an American industry more than three hundred years old. Its enforced wanderings are typical of the American appetite for raping the timber and the soil of one region and then moving on with a smack of the lips to the next virgin territory. It started in northern New England in the seventeenth century, and when the forests of New Hampshire and Massachusetts and Connecticut were tapped dry it moved down to the Carolinas and by the same ruinous process south into Georgia. When the Georgia trees were exhausted, down into Florida. 'A turpentine nigger' is in Florida a term of contempt. It is also the name of a mystery not one Floridian in a thousand has ever seen.

In the swampy interior the turpentine Negroes live in camps

and are supervised by a 'rider', a foreman on horseback, employed by the turpentine corporation. They seldom if ever come out of the jungle. They tap away for a few dollars a day, they produce children, often they are married, their women work with them. America to them is a small clearing for work, a fringe of dark pine, a two-room cabin in which they breed and die. Their life on this earth is at the disposal of the rider. He is the law, the good or bad provider, the judge of all their ways. They call him the Captain. Their drabness, their suppressed hopes, their sense of lowliness and sin are thoroughly purged once a week at what they call a jook party or tonk. These parties are the dim and little-known origin of the honky-tonk and the juke box. A Saturday night jook is a simple uninhibited orgy of drinking, dancing, singing, gambling, love-play, and occasionally knife-play in the pines outside. If you could have got into one of these jungles in the nineteen-thirties* you would have heard all that is most melancholy and desperate in the only indigenous American music – the blues. They cover every topic these people have heard of and all the work they or their kind have done. Blues about the pine tree that flowed gum till Judgement Day; about the lightning that struck the Captain down and freed them from the jungle; about John Henry, who in this version ran away to the Gulf Coast and made a kingly fortune plucking sponges from the ocean-bed with his naked hands. And when their special grievances are exhausted, they revert as country Negroes do everywhere in the South to the perpetual themes captured and taunted for all time in one tune, three lines of lyric, twelve bars of music: the song of people to whom life consists of a few riotous or appalling propositions – the need of a woman, the misery of a lover gone, the hope of a train to take you away from unhappiness, a train to bring you back to what is familiar and warm.

> When you see me comin', raise your window high,
> When you see me comin', raise your window high,
> But if you see me goin', hang yo' head and cry.

* They are now all but abandoned. A new process has transferred the work to large steam distilleries, which produce less folk-song but less misery.

And far from these jungles, wherever you go in inland Florida, you will hear against the weird sky the songs of Negroes. In the orange fields, pulling a sack from tree to tree, a fat girl shouts up to the bristling sun: 'Go down, Ol' Hannah, don't you rise no mo'.' By a railroad branch line near enough to the sea to taste a salt breeze, three Negroes squatting near the track hunched their shoulders and slapped their feet and sang:

> God rode out the ocean,
> Chained the lightnin' to his wheel;
> Stepped on land at West Palm Beach,
> And the wicked hearts did yield.

If you roam long and far enough you will begin to compose a picture of Florida whose symbol is no girl in an evening gown and a golden tan. You will come away from it with a memory of an old crone, around her neck the diamond necklace of Miami Beach, and for the rest a woman part Indian, part Negro, part Spanish, mostly Southern mountaineer; who grows oranges and smells of turpentine; who practises voodoo and smokes cigars; who counts cheap beads with her hands and keeps a union card in her pocket.

SPRING – BACKDROP FOR HISTORY

Anyone who talks about 'the American climate' is talking about something that does not exist. At various times of the year, somewhere on this continent are regions enjoying or enduring the climates of Naples and Morocco, of Iceland and Egypt, of Iran and Yorkshire and Norway and Switzerland and London and Yalta and Tibet.

Spring in America, you are often told, is a short drooling gasp between an Arctic winter and the stew of summer. This can be true of the North Atlantic seaboard and the Midwest but nowhere else. It is slow in the English way in Virginia, indolent and subtropical in Georgia and Louisiana, violent in New York, non-existent in Boston and interminable in Washington and Oregon. But in the northern third of the continental land-mass, you are likely to have in March or April a sudden splendour of sun and heat that brings the grass back again and has the dogwood and forsythia showering our rocky countryside and fetches the cherry-blossoms and the tourists to Washington.

It was on such a day that an Englishman walked into my office and said, 'You know, America has a fine crop of autumn flowers but is pretty poverty-stricken for spring flowers.' A week later another Englishman said to me, 'Of all the variety in America, there is no variety like that of spring flowers.'

The first man was making a generalization not about the spring but about himself. In the previous fall he had been two hundred miles away in up-state New York taking a holiday, tramping around and keeping his eyes open. But the rest of his two years here he had worked by day low down in a cement-and-steel canyon, and at night he lived high up in a cement-and-steel canyon. Neither in Wall Street nor on lower Fifth Avenue do magnolias or poinsettias burst up through the pavement. But the second man, who also works and lives in our man-made canyons, is one of those unconquerable Englishmen who on sunny Sundays is always taking buses, and where there are no buses he walks, being instantly recognizable as an Englishman on that score alone. And if there is a murky cloud and a hint of rain, then his nostrils open like those of the war-horses in the Bible. He grabs his trusty raincoat, heaves into a corner the 168 pages of the Sunday *New York Times*, the chronicle of the world's woes, and he goes out stalking really important things, poking among rocks for the exquisite jewel-weed, smiling without malice at the skunk cabbage, hailing the crocuses and feasting his soul on the thin golden stands of forsythia.

Springtime may be a date on a calendar, but the sure signs of it that coincide with this date in temperate countries come much sooner here, in some places, and much later in others. The children are still ski-ing to school in Vermont when the camellias are all over in Florida. And in one part of California, as everybody knows, one movie star fries by a desert swimming-pool and looks through field-glasses at another movie star ski-ing down a neighbouring mountain.

But suppose you started from New York in February, as it was once my unforgettable privilege to do, and drive south and west and up around the great curve of America west to Seattle. You would follow the slow-breaking marvel of the spring all the way. It was spring in Georgia at the end of February, and it was spring in the Cascades at the end of June. I went out of New York on a day of grey sleet and snow, and down to West Virginia I sloshed through valleys deep with snow and by mountain woods bare as combs. Two days later, in North Carolina, the pink-and-white dogwood made a cere-monial drive-way of the motor roads. In South Carolina I walked by a river which reflected banks of azaleas, white, lavender and scarlet. In Georgia the farmers paused often in the early morning to wipe their foreheads as they ploughed the red-clay fields. In Florida the tables were decorated with camellias. I should say that on the way I stopped and looked at several formal gardens, famous Southern gardens coming into luxurious flower: the neat formal gardens of Virginia, the lush tropical gardens of Mississippi. But I myself am not a great fan of the laid-out garden. The fact that somebody took the trouble to tame the landscape takes away for me the element of wonder. And when you walk around these places it is hard to distinguish between a native and an exotic. In such surroundings you are prepared for anything. But the never-ending delight of America in spring is the careless beauty, and the prodigal range, of the things that grow wild. Starting West from the west coast of Florida, I drove between a light green sea and flat sandy pineland. On my right for a hundred miles from Panama City to Pensacola was a continuous smear of a light, small pinkish flower. It was rosemary, brought here a hundred and eighty-eight years ago by a British soldier as a rare exotic. Now it is a pest.

On through Mobile, a smoky industrial port. But not all the conversion to war, and the reconversion, and the second reconversion can smother the azaleas rioting over factory walls and craning through the railings of the docks. You go on through dull scrub country, but you see pigs snuffling in the blossom of cypress swamps. In Texas, even along the flat and excruciating monotony of the eastern plain, bluebonnets race across the land like locusts. And along the banks of the streams and bayous the water hyacinth is as common as a dandelion in England.

We are still six hundred miles away from the American spring miracle – the Arizona desert. Most northern peoples, who look on a deciduous tree as the original anchor of reality, find something 'unnatural' in the trees of the tropics. They think of a desert as a yawning peril of sand and boredom between two habitable towns. But in southern Arizona in late February or early March the desert comes to flower. There is nothing on this earth to equal it. The prickly pear with flowers big as pineapples, the ocatilla with the tips of its branches dipped in scarlet, and the lowly enchantment of a plant that looks like what it's called – a hedgehog cactus – that bears a flower of a deep liquid fuchsia. You see these battalions of strange shapes (and cactuses are mostly named for their shape) flying their martial colours: the barrel cactus, the cotton-top, the grizzly bear, the pancake, the deer horn, the darning-needle, the beaver-tail. This is not all. Spring is not only the flowering of the erect cactuses. Between you and the fainting horizon is the scrub – the mesquite and cat's-claw and grease-wood and creosote and the grey-green sage. And pouring in and around these raw little islands are millions of humble wild-flowers, red and yellow and white and violet, washing across the sand for twenty miles or more to the purple mountains. This also is spring in America.

But to most of us it means trailing arbutus between the lakes and rocks of Maine; phlox and spring beauty and spring cabbage and bloodroot around New York; wild indigo in Georgia; laurel and Indian paintbrush through Texas; up in the farthest west, in northern Washington, whole mountain valleys shining with rhododendron. In California it is a thousand blooms, of everything that everybody else has and prizes for his own.

It is this season which, by a series of running coincidences, is at once the proudest and the most melancholy of American seasons. For against this setting, this shower of blossom and this promise of ripeness, Americans have known the worst and best of their history. That is another matter, and another talk.

SPRING – THE NINTH OF APRIL

Have you noticed how much more precious the spring is getting to be these years, or is it just an American feeling? I'm thinking of the beating monotone of anxiety through which we live our winters now. The wars and rumours of wars, the threat of spring invasions, the crises at the United Nations, the almost guilty hope that we can squeeze through another session of Congress and come out like the groundhog and the turtle to a lighter and more carefree time.

As the spring comes in the steam heat stops ticking in our radiators. The baseball teams end their winter training in Florida and Cuba, and grown men who argued through the winter about Korea and Tito and price control will daydream about the old Joe DiMaggio sinking back on his right knee and whamming a homer out of the ground.

In every country certain seasons stir the national memory of great events. The spring is such a time in America, and April especially. 'April is the cruellest month,' wrote an American poet, 'mixing memory and desire.' Lincoln was shot in April, and in April Franklin Roosevelt collapsed and died in Georgia. Every anniversary since that day a hard-bitten news agency has put out as an epitaph the great poem that Whitman wrote one year after the death of Lincoln, as the same forgotten flowers came up again: 'When lilacs last in the dooryard bloomed'. Most of all, though, we recall that the Civil War started and ended in April, and we cling in this age of violence a little wistfully to the last anecdote of that war, to the profound and civilized memory of the 9th of April, 1865. Because the Civil War was not only the first modern war but the last romantic war, and it ended on a note of that chivalry that used to be a code and now seems to have gone the way of jousting knights and Sir Walter Raleigh's cloak in the rain.

In the month before the end came, a northern army had

destroyed every growing thing in the Shenandoah Valley so that, as somebody said, 'a crow flying over it would have had to carry his own rations'. The southern armies were beaten, hungry, divided and deserting. The great army of Northern Virginia was down to twenty-five thousand men, bivouacked for the last night against odds of about nine to one. The last railroad that brought food to Lee's army was captured. On the night of the 8th, General Grant of the Union army had a sick headache and sat with his feet in hot water and mustard plasters on his neck. A mile or two away at Appomattox, Lee looked up to the high puffing clouds and saw the reflection of Grant's campfires on three sides. He sent a note to Grant to discuss peace but not to surrender. Grant had to refuse.

Next morning Lee decided to cut his way out. But the odds were hopeless and after a stiff fight against oncoming infantry and cavalry, Lee put out a white flag. At last the word got through to Grant, and his suspicious generals agreed to a two-hour all-quiet. And Lee's final surrender came through just before noon. Grant rode off to a little two-storey brick house by an apple orchard. Grant had never expected the end so soon and arrived at the place in a battle blouse, no coat, his trousers tucked into top-boots muddied from the ride. He was forty-two, with a black beard and an open shirt. He walked in and met the graceful idol of the South – a modest, erect, enormously handsome man of fifty-eight with a big upper body, brown liquid eyes, a fine head, greying hair, moustache and beard. Lee had put on a new dress uniform, a sash and sword. 'What his feelings were,' said Grant afterwards, 'I do not know ... he was a man of such dignity, with an impassable face.'* Grant himself had come at a gallop in high spirits, his headache gone. But he felt suddenly 'sad and depressed'.

They sat down and talked about old army times. It was so pleasant, and such a relief to Grant, that he forgot what he was there for till Lee gently reminded him. Grant thereupon asked for a pen and his old ledger and wrote in his own hand the ultimate terms – the surrender of the army of North-

* i.e. impassive

ern Virginia, all arms and artillery to be stacked. It occurred to him it would be a humiliation to ask for the surrender of side-arms. And it occurred also to the farm boy from Ohio, on a hint from Lee, that the Southern countryside would have to be worked again if the defeated were to eat and live. Thus he came to write in the noble sentence: 'Let every man of the Confederate army who claimed to own a horse or mule' take it home with him 'to work his little farm'. Lee bowed at the table and said this would have 'a happy effect' on his men. He rose to leave and hesitated. There was one other thing. His men, he said, had been without food for days and lived entirely off parched corn. Grant ordered rations for them all. The two men shook hands 'as cordially as we had met'. And it was all over. When the word got back to the Union lines, the men started letting off a salute of guns, and Grant stopped it.

So most of the Southerners went home. Many found their families lost, their homes burned and farms scorched, and wandered for a new life into Maryland, bringing, said a famous Marylander, 'no baggage save good manners and empty bellies'.

That is how the war ended, echoing in one clean encounter between the two commanders the marvellous clear trumpet promise of Lincoln's plea: 'Let us bind up the nation's wounds ... with malice towards none.'

And how did the conquered commander take this? He took it in the way that was his nature, with a solid, almost routine, knightliness. His traditional qualities no doubt live on, in professional soldiers I could name and you could name. And even in Ernest Hemingway's latest hero – for all his sour arrogance and fretting about his virility – the soldier's virtues of this dying tradition are taken for granted: magnanimity, respect for the enemy's humanity, obedience, chivalry to women.

Undoubtedly you have heard of Robert E. Lee, if only in the song about the steamboat that bore his name. But I should like to draw a little profile of him, since he is one of the great Americans of all time, and possibly one of the best human beings.

*

He was born into a Virginia family distinguished in public service since the time, only thirty years before, that two of its members had signed the Declaration of Independence. His father led Washington's cavalry and became the Governor of Virginia. But that was his all. He was a gay, impulsive, improvident man, and after a stretch in a debtors' prison he was mutilated in a riot, almost drowned in debt and managed to get himself marooned in the West Indies. He never saw his seven children again. Robert was brought up by an invalid mother until, at about the age of twelve, he had to 'carry the keys', as they said; that is, to order the food, watch after the dwindling moneys, and more or less bring up his mother. He went at eighteen to West Point, the United States Military Academy. He was gentle and very bright and came out second in his graduating year. He was put in the engineer corps and stayed there till he went off to the war with Mexico in 1846. He was then in his fortieth year. He served on the headquarters staff and got a strictly professional reputation for being tolerant of other people's convictions, for matching the enemy in surprise and outwitting them in manoeuvre. He went out as a colonel of cavalry into the Comanche country and came back in his fifties to settle at Arlington in Virginia as a professional soldier with some leisure, little money, several children and an ailing wife. He had long been depressed about the status of his slaves, of anybody's slaves, and he freed them. 'Slavery,' he wrote to his wife, 'is a moral and political evil in any country ... a greater evil to the white than the black.' Three years later he had the unpleasant job of capturing John Brown at Harpers Ferry and closing an underground railway into freedom with which as a man he was all in sympathy.

When the Civil War seemed inevitable, he was called back from service in Texas to Washington. It is one of the great ironies of military history that Lincoln, on the advice of a man who knew Lee's soldierly reputation, offered the command of the northern armies to Lee. He was then fifty-three, thirty-five years in the army, twenty-two years spent in moving up from captain to lieutenant-colonel; a dutiful, austere soldier of the Victorian sort, pretty much, he must have thought, at the end of his career. He could be the generalissimo of the Union. He had excellent grounds for rationalizing a natural ambition. He had freed his own slaves. He had said on record he could think of no calamity greater than the dissolution of the American Union. But he also thought the strength of the Union was in the freedom with which each state consented to be a part of it. No good, he said, would ever come of abolishing evil institutions at the point of the sword. Being Lee, he turned down the command and resigned his commission in the United States Army. At fifty-three, he was not a lieutenant-colonel. He was not even a soldier. He was a land-poor Virginian. 'If the Union is dissolved,' he wrote, 'I shall return to my native state and share the miseries of my people and save in defence I will draw my sword on none.' That is what he did. Within weeks, Virginia had seceded. And he offered himself to the army of Virginia.

This is not the place to talk of his military brilliance. He revolutionized the defensive position. He started always from an outnumbered corps and by supple and unpredictable manoeuvre kept a huge enemy stretching its superior supply lines like the spokes of a wheel. In the end, he had neither the men, the supplies, the food, the ships nor the mobility to prevent the enemy's choosing the place for the showdown.

He has remained through all the intervening years the sainted hero of the South. Which may or may not be a good thing. For it is shocking to see some of the people who worship him: professional Southerners still chewing on the cud of a dead grievance; formidable dames who band together to use Lee's reputation for bigoted ends; people who still exploit his memory as a curse on all his enemies and throw organized apoplexies whenever some historian makes the simple, true statement that the meeting at Appomattox is memorable for the magnanimity of Grant. 'Biographies of Lee,' says a stern New England historian, 'tend to sentimentality.' So they do. But Lee himself tended, as much as any soldier ever did, to sainthood. He was the same when things went well or badly. He retreated in order with the wounded accounted for. He set his own alarming standards for his generals: not only of duty and resolution, but of gentleness. He went in to retrieve, with-

out blame, men who had acted and failed on their own initia-
tive. He stood up always in the presence of enlisted men. He
never was known to lose his temper, but unlike some other self-
controlled Victorians he did not take this out on his subordinates by the terror of his example. He ended his days as a
college President. He sat in his broken countryside and saw the
carpetbaggers swarm over it, and chided any student who got
mad at them or railed at the Negroes' new and sometimes
aggressive freedom. He begged money for poor students and
simply took their note of hand when the money couldn't be
raised. His hair and beard were white now. As he walked in his
erect way around the town, with his massive head and his fine
eyes, people thought they saw God go by. He could have had
a weeping mob at his heels any time and called the turn of
vengeance or resistance. He sensed this and kept indoors. He
refused to run as Governor of Virginia because 'my nomination
would be injurious to the state'.

I can think of other Victorians who seem much like him,
upright 'Christian gentlemen', as they were called, who, the
more you learn about them, turn more and more into graceful
monsters. I can find none of this in Lee. He was happiest with
children, kindest to the humble and the man in the ranks, most
patient with most stupid lieutenants. He never preached and he
disliked speeches. But even a devoted Southerner has said the
trouble with him is 'the monumental quality of his virtuous-
ness'. You look at the warm humorous eyes and the generous
mouth and it doesn't seem possible. But wait. In the military
textbooks you will find a fault. This is the dread sentence the
West Point Cadets learn about him: 'He had a tendency to
trust his subordinates too much and an unwillingness to force
his decisions on them.'

There is nothing much to build on there. I'm afraid he was
simply a great and very good man. And if there was anything
rigid about him, it was the assumption natural to his day that
the saving grace of war was the daily exercise of chivalry. It
makes you wonder whether this type in our day – any day
after the invention of the flame thrower and the jelly bomb
– could ever be a successful soldier.

AMERICAN SUMMER

Of the four American seasons none is more dramatic or more humbling than the summer. It is a time when heat-waves roam around the continent moody as bandits, and close in on unsuspecting places, on southern swamps and midland prairies and northern valleys, with thunder out of the Apocalypse and a one-night respite of cool after rain. Then they gather their forces and are off again after another victim.

Only in Maine and down most of the Pacific Coast can you be sure of cool grey days. Only in western Oregon is the grass green and knee-high all the time. And the price they pay is the English price: cloudy skies, gentle showers spoiling tennis games and picnics, and a breed of sober people who expect the worst and live in raincoats. But everywhere else the summer is a blinding ordeal that drains off the fierce American energy; it takes a lot of the brashness out of them, leaving them a little more limp and a little more lovable. In the South it is so surely the fate of every man, every year, that they pretend to make a virtue of it. There is hardly one of the state guide-books that does not discover, with a little cheer of surprise, a compensation in the climate the stranger would never suspect. Thus, although 'Louisiana has a semi-tropical climate ... [it] is remarkably equable over large areas.' Texas starts in with the brazen sentence: 'Texas climate is remarkable for its salubrity,' and adds the insult, 'the summer heat is surprisingly bearable'. And Mississippi turns a barefaced lie into a boast with the final sentence: 'This almost sub-tropical climate not only makes for pleasant living, but assures approximately a nine-month growing season.'

Several times I have had the misfortune to be in the Southwest in midsummer, and once I was going through the Great American desert. A small town that lies there, in the Imperial Valley, is a marketing centre called El Centro. It is below sea-level. Its gardens are always in flower, but only because they are irrigated, for they have there about three inches of rain a year. Most of the year you would have trouble snapping pictures of the inhabitants, and in summer it would be next to impossible. For they cling like lizards to the deep shade of the hangovers, or arcades, that are built over the store-fronts and run from the top of the first storey high across the sidewalk. El Centro is on that highway which, when it was only a path, was well christened by the early Spanish priests the Journey of Death, or the Devil's Highway. Only a few miles to the south are beds of fossilized oystershells, and petrified fish left there when this bone-dry region was an ocean bed. El Centro, you will gather, is out of this world and ought to stay there. At three in the afternoon the houses and stores glowed pink with heat and the desert beyond was a white glare to bruise the eyes. It was 118 degrees in the shade. But when I asked a policeman if it would be quicker to drive to the coast by a northern route going through another inferno called Indio, he looked at me in a tender sort of alarm. 'Say,' he said, 'if you want to stay comfortable, better keep out of Indio. That is one hot town.'

Here, patrolling the Journey of Death, he felt just the same gratitude as people in Brittany, Florida, Manchester and Glasgow for having been born there instead of anywhere else. It shows at least that most people have a natural determination to hang on. I staggered away from the cop, put a dime in a slot machine, took out a packet of salt pills and swallowed a couple.

But the midsummer has compensations the guide-books don't mention. The Russians and food prices suddenly seem less exhausting than the weather. The brisk regiments of middle-aged females who are always signing you up for crusades on behalf of lost causes – homeless cats, say, or the Republicans – call off the route march and retire to a summer porch and beakers of grapefruit juice. The summer forces you back on the more primitive crafts of staying alive. So in summer Britons and Americans are farther apart, though in an innocent way, than at any other time of the year. Even socialites and intellectuals stop trying to be like other socialites and intellectuals, and fall back on the customs of the country, and so do again the unpretentious things of their childhood.

It is natural that summer should remind you of childhood because it is the ways of childhood that are the essential folkways. And it follows that the summer is the time which brings on in the exile the acutest attacks of homesickness. For then he is surrounded by customs, precautions and proverbs that are different from his own. And a man is not apt to know what he likes most in his native land until he misses it. In my early days here I used to think often of English summers: the heavy dew on the grass in the morning and the rising mist; the rush for the morning paper to see what Hobbs or Hammond was doing in the Test Match; the smell of linseed on a cricket bat and the smell of sweat on abandoned – what's the word? – sweaters; the taste of cocoa and sugar mixed in a paper bag to take on bicycle rides; the forgotten raincoat and the fine rain coming on and the retreat to a fat oak; picking hips and haws off hedgerows; walking along canal banks on Sunday evenings; putting on a tweed coat and playing bowls, bowls, bowls; snatching at your parents' advice to get in a healthy walk and tearing off to the Blackpool promenade to spark the girls; paying a more literal attention to the parents' advice about climbing over stiles and watching out for nettles.

You might think that everybody who speaks a form of English knows what a nettle is. I once conducted a private poll of the Americans nearest to hand: the men and girls who work in the New York office of the B.B.C. I asked simply, 'What is a nettle?' Out of ten people, only three had a fair idea. Two admitted they didn't know. Another said, 'It's some sort of fly or bug, isn't it?' A fourth thought it grew in wheat. A research man came back smartly with, 'It's a horticultural product, but don't ask me what.' A conscientious library assistant who hates to let you down thought, 'It's sort of being on edge, but I couldn't exactly define how or what.' Another research man knew the line about 'this nettle danger' and ascribed it to Neville Chamberlain.

In this country the far more perilous equivalent is poison ivy, on the West Coast poison oak. Whatever facts of life are left out of a baby's education, not many Americans are unacquainted at a tender age with the little three-leafed monster that grows everywhere and touched by the bare skin puts you in bed and in agony, inflates you to the texture of a blimp and makes your skin an obscene imitation of rhinoceros hide. My six-year-old is well trained. 'Look out for poison ivy,' he replied when I asked him what summer meant to him. 'No,' I said, 'I mean just summer; what do you do in summer?'

'Oh,' and his face cleared, 'you go naked, go swimming, smash pennies on the railroad track, catch swell-bellies and have lots of fun.' Since you don't have to climb down to American railway tracks, it's a regular thing, when guests are coming or going, to put a penny on the track before the train comes in and see Lincoln obliterated when it has gone. Swell-bellies, I ought to say, are a pest-fish we catch around Long Island. They are more elegantly known as blowfish, due to their habit of blowing themselves into a balloon when they taste a hook. They, or rather the one slim fillet of fish that lies along their backbone, are also sold in the more refined restaurants under the expensive title of 'sea squab'.

To other children summer means getting your father to buy you a new baseball bat; sneaking a little tar from the men repairing the roads and going off and setting fire to a corner lot, and appointing the boldest boy to phone the fire department. Summer is the brown, frowzy grass everywhere. It's the pungent whiff of skunk as your car turns a bend on a summer evening. It's the mid-afternoon jaunt to the drugstore and the merciful suffocation of an ice-cream soda. It's week-ends slathering a new and smellier suntan oil on your body. It's the fire-hydrants turned on in city streets and naked youngsters prancing like plucked chickens into the torrent. It's the still evenings in the big cities, hot as open ovens, and the big sullen ball of sun smouldering into the rivers. It's the enchanting women, the weaving long-legged American women, the tanned shoulders and glistening figures gliding casually through streets and hotels and movies and parks.

These are what an adult sees and remembers. But before he has time to stroll and look around there are things he has to do. Before the summer comes on he has to fix the door- and window-screens to save the family from the insect *Luftwaffe* that is let loose on the human race in these parts. Certainly horse-flies are bigger here, and mosquitoes are nimbler, but I'm not sure that Americans are more plagued with house-flies and winged insects than Britons are. They won't tolerate them indoors with the same phlegm.

Then there's the buffalo moth, a ferocious beast that sets the housewife in the spring sending off the family's winter uniforms to the cleaners, getting them back and into zipper bags, and hanging moth-ball tins in cupboards and setting off bombs of D.D.T. in dark closets. If your child has tonsillitis, you get his tonsils out before the first of June, for the mid-summer months are the most dangerous for infantile paralysis; and it is well-authenticated that tonsillitis convalescents are push-overs for the dreaded bug. (In America, a germ is a bug, an insect is a bug; a bedbug is a bedbug.)

When all these things are done, you are protected as well as you ever can be from the coming onslaught. Then the first heat descends. And some people get browner, and middle-aged people get yellower, and old people get whiter. And by the beginning of August there is only a month to go before the great trek back to a regular office life and another winter's grind, and the Russians. So people abandon themselves with a little less conscience than usual to week-end play, to county fairs, and hay-rides, and beach parties, and night baseball, played under blinding floodlights that make baseball look like a game invented by Orson Welles. In the East there are horse shows and dog shows and archery tournaments and sailing; in the South watermelon-eating competitions, and racing after greased pigs, and the more general debauch of expiring on porches. In the Midwest more fairs and yacht races; and out West rodeos, and huckleberry feasts, and trout-catching contests, and fiestas recalling the Spanish days, and much solemn growing of beards by bank presidents and garage mechanics to honour the pioneers, who stayed hairy simply because it cost a week's wage to get a shave.

At this time of the year about twenty-odd million Americans are living in some other place than home: in summer camps by lakes, in cottages by the Atlantic; or driving through the forests and deserts and over the mountains, going through the vast National Parks, looking for the America they have read about – the continent of the pioneer trails, of national memorials, the route of Lincoln's walk into Illinois, the place where De Soto first saw the Mississippi, the rude bridge at Concord and Thoreau's little backyard universe.

All these are festivals of the white man. But in one bare and blinding region of America, in the South-west, August is the month of the red man. And in the last two weeks the red man beats and patters over the ground in religious ceremonies that go on for seven and nine days at a time. In the third week in August, in four separate pueblos in New Mexico, you can see a dance that is as old a ritual as any on this continent. It is the corn dance. And down in Arizona the Hopis are doing their rain dance.

We had better understand right away what I mean by corn. I remember, a few years ago, visiting an old Englishman in Hertfordshire. An American girl was along (with me, I should say), and when with a wave of his arm the old man indicated a field of wheat and remarked that the corn was doing well that year, the girl said, 'Oh, so *this* is what you call corn.'

'This,' he said with a piercing look, '*is* corn.'

Well, I am glad to tell you (via the *Encyclopaedia Britannica*) that corn is no specific crop, but is used locally to describe the staple crop, whatever it happens to be. Thus in England it may be wheat, but in Scotland it's oats, and in the United States it's what you call maize, and what Americans a long time ago called Indian corn and now just 'corn'. A field of ripe corn in America is a field of green stems, sprouting yellow-brown tassels. They are head high, like wilting swords. Ruth 'amid the alien corn' would have felt even more alien in Iowa.

If it had not been for the corn they found growing here, the early colonists on this coast would have perished. But the Indians had developed a most elaborate method of growing it, choosing the right ground, fertilizing it, protecting the seed, planting it with various combinations of vegetables, and exploiting many ways of harvesting it, storing it, grinding it, and cooking it. If the corn crop was ruined, it might be the end of that tribe. You may recall how Hiawatha struggled with the maize god.

The deserts of the South-west are Indian country for a brutally simple reason. Only the Indian can manage to survive there and coax every drop of the rare, rare rain, or water channelled from distant floods, into careful terraces that grow his corn, beans and melons on soil that is mostly sand. The Indian tribes were exterminated in most of the gentler climates where the white man could settle – and shoot. But in the Arizona desert the Hopi Indians are periodically amused by the efforts of government experiments to farm. They have always failed. If the Government would like to learn, the Hopis would be glad to teach. Somebody, commenting on the government policy towards the Indians, remarked that 'they put the Indian on lands where a white man would starve. They expected him to starve, but he fooled them.'

The Hopi tribe is the thriftiest group of Americans alive, perhaps because they inhabit the most barren and God-forsaken stretch of landscape on this continent. It is a reservation in the north-east corner of Arizona, about a hundred and fifty miles east of the Grand Canyon. The annual rainfall, a guide once said, 'is equivalent to spitting in the Grand Canyon'.

The Hopis live in villages on the tops of mesas.* Their form of society is a matriarchy: that is to say, the woman owns the house and the man goes to work after marriage on the fields that are his wife's property. There is an old English belief that this is true of all American society, but I should say, in the cause of accuracy, that I am now talking about the Hopi Indians of Arizona. Their need of water is so urgent and so ancient that much of their religion has to do with rituals and ceremonies designed to persuade the gods to send rain.

Towards the end of August they enact their nine-day Snake Dance. No white man, or any other visitor, is allowed to see what goes on the first eight days. But on the ninth day a few score tourists, assured by the Chamber of Commerce that what they are going to see is something secret, if not obscene,

* Little mountains with a flat top.

113

bang over a dirt road for a hundred miles and stand around panting in the ruthless sun. Then the dance begins.

Nearly naked figures, painted and feathered, troop into a little plaza and shower it with sacred meal – corn. These are the snake priests. They join the antelope priests, with white legs and furred skins. They begin to chant. There is no music, and no other accompaniment than some rattles they carry. They sway and rock around the circle till one of them breaks it and goes to its centre, where there is a little pile of brush. He plucks from it a rattlesnake. The others follow him and do the same. The dancers break into a rhythmic jog, swaying from side to side with their trunks down, like a lost battalion shot in the stomach. The snakes are writhing around their necks, over their arms, girdling their waists. You notice now that a drum-beat punctuates a little sense for Western ears into their moaning chant. The rattling sound grows finer and more intense, and the panting tourists notice, with much more alarm than the priests, that it is coming this time from the snakes themselves. By all the laws of biology and survival, the snakes should now strike and kill.

I never met anybody who for certain saw it happen. When all the snakes are out of the brush, the head priest scatters a ring of corn on the ground, and the snakes are dropped into it. Then the dancers bless the snakes, seize one or two and rush off to the edge of the mesa. There the snakes are set free and left to slide away to the horizon and intercede with the gods for rain. Sometimes the rain does come. Other times it does not. The newspapers argue. The Indians are wounded to the quick. White men who never entered a church become hang-dog believers. Scientists testily explain that the snakes have been plucked of their sting. Meteorologists say that the air-currents are such in mid-August in that part of the country that an inch of rain is a safe bet. All I know is that sometimes there is rain, sometimes there is not.

But the white man gaping on is paying a tribute of his own, of a sort. He has come in his automobile, his digestion busy with some satisfying frozen foods, to stand in awe for a little while before a dramatization of the original American tragedy: the pitiful prayer to God to water the earth and

114

make something grow to eat. He is seeing his first American host, who greeted him three hundred years ago with kindness and who still survives, in the blinding lunar landscape the white man banished him to, living out what is supposed to be the regular American challenge: the response of a brave man to Nature in the raw. Well, the Hopis are, in the words of a shrewd geographer, still living the heroic age, 'the period of direct contact with Nature'. Year in, year out, they do as a routine what none of the spectators could improvise in the desperation of desert hunger. If we are going to get into the swing of these times, and apply the acid test to everyman's Americanism, we should strike a medal for the Hopis, the only extant one hundred per cent Americans.

THE FALL OF NEW ENGLAND

There are times of the year when anybody with an itch for travel must think of those parts of the earth that God favoured above all others when He handed out the seasons. There are two of these that I have enjoyed many times but I still find myself goggling and marvelling every time they come around. One is the English spring and the other is New England in the fall.

The best of English poets have celebrated the rich, sombre English autumn, but an American fall bears little resemblance to that 'season of mists and mellow fruitfulness'. Many famous Britons have put on record their astonishment at the youthful, trumpeting quality of the fall, at the hot days and the Mediterranean blue skies encircling a landscape of blinding scarlet and gold. Lord Bryce, not a reticent man about American vices, couldn't trust his English reserve to speak properly about its virtues. Lloyd George confessed after his only trip to America that no matter how inconclusive his political mission had been he would at least go home remembering the overwhelming experience of the fall. A hundred years ago, Mrs Trollope, who liked very little about these United States, broke down and wrote that at this season of the year 'the whole country goes to glory'.

The fall ranges throughout the whole hardwood or deciduous region of the country, from the north woods of Maine clear across the Midwest as far as the Dakotas and way down South to the foothills of the Rockies in Texas. Since no American can bear to believe that he or his parents chose a second-rate place to be born in, there is no agreement about where the fall is at its best. The residents of the Great Lakes say that no sumacs flame like their sumacs. And the pride of a man from Arkansas in his blazing hawthorn trees is a wild grab at plucking a virtue out of necessity. A native of another land can simply report that the fall of New England is as a four-alarm fire to a lighted match. There is no way to describe it or talk about it, except in the language of Milton and Shakespeare, who never saw it.

But it is possible to say why it's so. Everybody enthuses about the fall but nobody explains it. It is due to a happy accident of climate, a steady brilliance of October sun going to work on the great variety of American hardwoods and the fairly arid soil they stand in. The superiority of New England's fall – of that in Vermont, New Hampshire and Massachusetts especially – is due to their latitude. These states are far enough north to get an early cold spell to quicken the sap before the prolonged sunshine of October brings it out as colour in the leaves. They are far enough south to escape a continuous and withering frost, which is what nips the Canadian fall before it can come to its prime. Farther south – in Pennsylvania, Maryland, Virginia and the Carolinas – they get no cold, except at high altitudes, and by the time the sap is forced up and ready for showing off, the leaves are crumbling and falling.

In most temperate countries the strong pigments that have been hidden from view in the greens of summer never do come out, because the autumn brings in rain and mists and threatening grey skies. The whole trick of the New England fall is nothing more complicated than that of a photographic negative handled by a superior developer. In the autumn, the countrymen tell us, the sap is blocked from the leaf by a new growth of hard cells at the base of the twig. So the greens fade. Now all you need is an October of brilliant light and warmth to develop out the yellows and the reds. The only other qualification is a lack of rain. On rich and rainy soils like those of England the leaves stay green too late till the frost kills them. New England, on the contrary, has many causes to lament its rather poor soils. But it never regrets them in the fall, for their very lack of nitrogen stimulates a great range of yellows and golds. And the acid in the leaves is what burns them scarlet. The fall, then, is nothing more than the thorough burning out of what is poor in the soil and what is bitter in the leaf. 'It is,' says Donald Culcross Peattie, 'essentially death that causes all the brave show.' But it is a fierce and productive death.

I once went north from New York City at the very beginning of the fall to meet the peak of it wherever it might be between Maine and southern Connecticut. The first signal of the glory to come is a bare tree, which is never bare until the fall is ready to ripen. It is the butternut tree, and it sheds everything just as the bushes and berries are beginning to trickle out their purple. By the green edge of the parkway on which I was driving, little piles of brown leaves, already dead, lay at the foot of hickory trees. The ferns were dry. The bracken and blueberry bushes were wine dark, the sumac a throbbing vermilion. Everywhere there was the smell of burning wood, letting off violet wisps of smoke to smear the cloudless sky – like trickles of milk on window panes.

At this point I wanted to take off my glasses, which a notation on my driving licence forbids. This is another thing about the fall. The sparkling clarity of the light gives to short-sighted people the constant sense that their eyesight has marvellously improved and that they are seeing fences, barns, steeples and billboards in the sharp outline they probably have for other people all the time.

I drove up and over the hills across from New York State into Connecticut, past roadside stands piled high with jugs of cider and pyramids of pumpkins. And then I started to follow a river whose banks were black with stands of evergreen. By now a green field was just another daub on the crowded palette of the landscape. We were still far from the fall's peak. It was still the small, treeless things that were trying to be splendid. The briar and bushes and vines were sparkling. I do not know them well enough to single out their separate charms, but it is an annual joy to see brush which most of the time is a mesh of old wire suddenly disclose a jewel of a flower. Pokeweed, and pitchpine cone, and unpretentious things like partridge berry and jack-in-the-pulpit. All of them have a special shining berry, a bursting husk, a momentary bloom.

I got out of the car and wallowed in the silence and the

singing colour and the balmy heat. At the rim of my tyre I noticed that the smooth white cement of the highway had cracked under the tension of a cranberry vine. And through this crack, and edging into the highway, wild cranberries grew. I looked ahead at the engineered boulevard of the highway, pouring like two ribbons of toothpaste to the horizon, quite heedless of its defeat by the concentrated violence of a tiny and delicate vine. That just about put industrial know-how in its proper place. And I climbed back and went on, warming to the excitement of what was to come.

And now the trees took over. After another twenty miles, the evergreens came in thick and fast. Even a pine looked like a new invention seen in its inkiness against a flaming maple. Now I was surrounded by two other properties that make the New England fall unique. First and above all the maple, with its bursting sugar which blazes into scarlet. And then the oaks. An Englishman is surprised to wonder about many slender trees and hear them called oaks. The fat old oak tree of England, with his legs planted solidly on lush damp ground, is a rare sight. But New England has a teeming variety of oaks, and their value as a spectacle is that in the fall they entirely revise your ideas about the infinite fine range of colour between gold and lemon. And beside this perpetual shower of scarlet and lemon and gold, the white birches slid by like slivers of mercury. And rising from the foam of every valley, slim as thermometers, were the white spires of Colonial churches, keeping count of the general fever. I had hit the peak, and the state of our language being what it is, in my hands at least, there is no more point in going on about it in prose. Some great composer might convey the majesty of it. Only a child in ecstasy could hit off the youth and hilarity of it. For children are natural impressionists, taking the adjectives of music and knifing them close against the nouns of sight and touch. Every child knows that colour sings and trees walk. But puberty is the end. They acquire the logic that is death to the spirit and life to what is called maturity, and like the rest of us repress the wild energy of their instinctive knowledge. And so we can only guess at the form of art in which perhaps some hundreds of years from now the New England fall will come to be represented. I would take a bet that, by our present resources, Cézanne and Handel together might give a fair account of it. For the present I can only tell you that the fall is wonderful in life and awful in painting.

In this setting you can find an American life, proud but not prosperous, that also seems doomed to die in the industrial democracy that surrounds it. Don't imagine that the small village I am taking you into, in the south of Vermont, is typical of New England today. It is typical of nowhere else, but New England is many things besides small memorials to the declining eighteenth century. The New England puritan of English stock has not been the typical New Englander for two generations. Sixty per cent of the people in the six states of New England have at least one parent foreign born, against only five per cent in the Southern states. Today the Connecticut Yankee has only one chance in three of being, like the first settlers, a Protestant with an English name. It's two to one that he's an Italian or a Pole, and a wise newspaper editor once warned me to take for granted that any stranger I met on the streets of New England was a Catholic. To make certain that what I am going to talk about, though once radical and typical in New England, is now conservative and odd, I should also warn you that the typical Yankee is no longer a farmer. In 1790, ninety-seven New Englanders in every hundred lived on the land, and three in towns. In 1870, it was still only twenty-one townsfolk against seventy-nine countrymen. Today in the United States, fifty-six per cent of the people live in cities. In New England, seventy-seven per cent of the entire population lives in cities, only twenty-three per cent in the country. So New England is the most industrialized of all American regions. If this shocks you, it would shock most Americans more, for they stubbornly think back to New England as the source and replenisher of all their canniest and most down-to-earth virtues.

Bearing in mind, then, that we are looking at a tiny green spot in the upper right-hand corner of the turbulent industrial landscape of the north-eastern states, let's take a look at the sort of place that bred New England. It is a small valley six miles long and two miles wide. You might say that it was bound by mountains, but to a Westerner they would be low, well-wooded hills, for the hills that enclose this valley are nowhere higher than a thousand feet. Yet the valley is more fertile than most places in Vermont, with grass for summer pasture and winter hay. It grows corn and perhaps a crop of oats. And the farmer's cash in the bank comes from the one cow a year he sells. To a stranger it would look like good sheep country, and so it would be if there weren't out West the vast hills of Montana and Wyoming and Colorado to make it hardly worth while for a Vermonter to breed them. Then, there's so much rock and boulder in the hills of Vermont that by now the oldest Vermont joke tells how the sheep have their noses sharpened so they can get at the grass (God anticipated the plight of Vermont by making sheep with cleft lips).

If you were to motor along this valley, and your car had some sort of trouble, a quiet hard-bitten Vermonter would in time – his time – appear and tinker awhile and in the end put it right. He wouldn't say a word. And you'd have to be an outlander to try and pay him in any way. For Vermonters, settled long ago on a poor soil, and used to winters that hold more snow than the Arctic, don't expect a smiling face from Nature and don't reflect it in themselves. An Englishman coming here and going straight to Vermont and expecting to meet casual, backslapping people would be in for a ghastly surprise. A man is a stranger there up to the third and fourth generation. And the only reliable way they have of placing a face or a name is to ask who his mother was. (His father simply served his mother's turn.) It's been said that Vermonters look on life as a necessary struggle against evil, a struggle you must make and expect to lose. It's also the only state in the United States where you will hear the word 'thrift' used all the time. They never throw anything away. In a little booklet about this valley I am talking about, written by a couple of natives, you will read this sentence: 'The people are friendly and always willing to help a neighbor. This means more to us who live here than material wealth, which none of us possess.' To walk into the centre of this village of Newfane, you would never believe it. It is a handsome common with a couple of shops, an inn and a quite magnificent courthouse. The town was settled in 1776, but the county courthouse didn't go up until fifty years later, and we can be thankful for that. For in the interval Americans conceived a passion for everything Greek. Believing that they had just successfully established the first genuine democracy since the Greeks and the grandest Republic since Rome, they took to naming their town with classical names. Hence Philadelphia, Annapolis, Laconia, Athens, Sparta, Seneca, Cicero, Troy. Thomas Jefferson built a home with a columned portico. And soon country courts, and inns, and farmhouses were doing the same. It may sound like a dubious fad, but Americans stuck to their preference for wooden houses, and today New England is glorified with hundreds of churches, houses, courthouses, the wood painted white, with pillared porticos and graceful spires. In this small village in Vermont, the county courthouse is an exquisite symbol of what Americans did in wood with Greek forms.

Opposite the courthouse is the inn, which is also the jail. Newfane has kept up its habit of feeding its prisoners from the inn, and since the inn serves the best food around here, it's sometimes hard to get the inmates out of jail. Theodore Roosevelt said he would like to retire here, commit some 'mild crime' and eat his way through a cheerful old age.

If you went along the valley you would be walking without knowing it through another town called Brookline, for Brookline is simply the scattered houses of the valley. It has less than a hundred people, mostly farmers, and they are their own rulers. Its first town meeting was held in 1795 and the last one was held last week. The names at the first meeting are still there: Moore and Waters, and Ebenezer Wellman and Cyrus Whitcomb, and Christopher Osgood (there has always been a Christopher on the Osgood farm). Walking along the road you might run into the tractor of a Mr Hoyt. He is to all intents a farmer. And so he is. He is also the road commissioner of the valley. His wife, Minnie Hoyt, is the town clerk, a justice of the peace, and when she isn't doing the farming chores she's busy signing fishing licences, or marrying a visiting couple, or telling the comfortable city-people who have made a summer home here that by decision made at the last town meeting their taxes will be twice as much next year. What is striking to an Englishman here is that the few fairly well-to-do people are all what they call 'summer folks', people who made a farm over as a summer retreat from New York or Boston. But the summer folks are strangers and underlings. The valley has heard many delicate sounds through the years. But it has never heard the advice of a squire or the accent of *noblesse oblige*. The farmers are ruled and rulers. The wealthy stranger goes cap in hand and pays his rates according to Minnie Hoyt and does what Mr Hoyt says to keep his part of the highway safe and sound.

Our pilgrimage ends with an odd little building, a round schoolhouse. It was put up in the eighteen-twenties and is shaped like a silo, just one room with five windows equally spaced in a circle around it. It was so built, they say, because at that time the valley lived in fear of a highwayman called 'Thunderbolt', whom no one had ever seen. The schoolmaster, a Scot from Muirkirk, one Dr Wilson, had his desk facing the door and could see through all the windows the first approach of any robber, or of the dreaded Thunderbolt. Thunderbolt's presence seemed to have haunted the valley for a couple of decades, but one gets a reassuring picture of Yankee vigilance in the dour figure of Dr Wilson, spelling out his lessons to the valley children and in the twilight letting his fingers play on the barrel of his shotgun as his protective eye rolled around the five windows.

I leave you with this comforting image of the rude forefathers of today's New Englanders. Having led you so far into a mystery, though, it occurs to me you may wonder if they ever caught Thunderbolt. Yes, they did.

When the good Dr Wilson died they took off the high scarf he always wore and on his neck they saw scars and the marks of chains. Sure enough, HE was Thunderbolt.

SIREN SOUNDS

The Police Commissioner of New York and the civilian defence officials have decreed that because of the historic peril in which we all stand a most un-American silence must fall over the city. There must be no sirens sounded until the bombs begin to fall. This ruling does not promise merely the absence of noise, but the absence of an everyday hundred per cent American noise: the noise of a police siren.

A police siren does not sound like Moaning Minnie or even like the air-raid sirens we used during the last war in our practice black-outs. Many of you will have heard it in the movies. It is a high-graduated scream, moaning into your ken and swooping off into the distance again like an angry wife with ten-league boots on. Almost any evening in Manhattan, when you are sitting home with a book, and there is no sound but the peevish exhaust of the radiator going 'Tooo-phut!' you will suddenly become aware of a sound so distant and ethereal that it might be a radio amateur oscillating your set. But it comes on nearer, modulates to a whimper, growls at a traffic light and is soon shrieking almost inaudibly a couple of miles away. When you hear it you make an idle guess at which of three events it might be signalling. It could be a police car dashing up to the Bronx to save one Irishman from another in Joe's saloon. It might be a fire-engine, and most people throw open the windows at that thought, because nobody ever grows out of the lust for seeing fires. It might be a city official late for an appointment, or a distinguished visitor being whisked by police escort to catch the *Queen Mary*.

The first time I ever heard it was in Hollywood, California, one balmy night after a summer of no rain at all, and daily warnings from the Mayor of Los Angeles, the conservation department and the forestry service that the forests, on the mountains that look down to the Pacific, were now so brittle that one careless match could transform Hollywood from a purgatory into an inferno. I was walking along Wilshire Boulevard, and the withering sound came piercing through the sky and the palm trees. Well, this was it. Instinctively people turned inland and looked to the mountains. But it came roaring right past us and stayed on level ground. It was merely two policemen on motor-bikes escorting a long, black car. I learned later there was no fire, no accident, no brawl. It was Jean Harlow on her way to a nightclub.

The week before a presidential election is the worst of all, a banshee convention from dawn to midnight. The sirens howl while the Democratic candidate is borne to a speech in Union Square, while the Republican candidate is hurled up to Harlem and back to his hotel. There's no doubt that it's a very effective way of cowing any kind of traffic, causing even cab drivers, who normally bounce their cars against a rude colleague, to skulk over against the sidewalk.

As a stranger here you would doubtless be baffled by all this pother and exhibitionism. Why can't the candidate start earlier? Must distinguished visitors wait longer than other people to pack their bags for the voyage? And why a police escort? Why must the President whizz through a city in the middle of a covey of cops on motor-cycles, and how about the solid little men riding the running-boards, their snap brims tugged over one eye, their shoulders bunched, their right hands ominously in their pockets? Who do they think they are, Humphrey Bogart? They are the most conspicuous convoy ever assembled, yet they are known as the Secret Service. Even this information doesn't impress the English visitor, although he admittedly spends half his time in America hoping American life is like the movies and the other half hoping it isn't. What, he asks, is so vulnerable about a President, a visiting statesman, a movie star? The Prime Ministers of Great Britain are not noticeably a tougher breed of men. And the King of England is not less precious to his people than the President of the United States. Indeed, he was once thought to be divine. But he travels at an easy pace in an open car with no one on the running-board. And the Prime Minister goes unheralded by these mechanical howls of pain. The faintly contemptuous Briton, if he can make his voice heard against the siren's tip-off to all intending assassins that the great man is coming within range, will add the final reminder that in Britain policemen do not carry pistols.

The answer is short and humiliating. How often has anybody taken a pot-shot at a Prime Minister? The sad truth is that three modern Presidents – Lincoln, Garfield and McKinley – were shot and killed while in office. In Miami in 1933, the Mayor of Chicago got fatally in the way of a bullet intended for Franklin Roosevelt. And in November 1950, Harry S. Truman would certainly have met his fate had it not been for the fortunately witless bungling of a couple of Puerto Ricans.

The United States secret service was organized in the July after Lincoln was shot in his box at Ford's Theatre on that April night of 1865. But that misfortune had nothing to do with it. The original purpose of the secret service can be guessed at in its creation as a special division of the United States Treasury. It was set up to suppress counterfeiting. There was then no standard national paper money. Banks did their own printing, according to something like three thousand various designs. A man might get to be a millionaire on currency of his own invention, and many a man tried. Not until 1901, when President McKinley was shot up in Buffalo, New York, did the secret service assign some of its men to protect the succeeding President, Theodore Roosevelt, and not until four years later did Congress appropriate the money for the particular purpose of protecting 'the person of the President of the United States, the members of his immediate family, and of the person chosen to be President'. Today the secret service has three duties: to go after smugglers and counterfeiters, to track down income-tax evaders, and to protect the President and the President-elect. The First World War dramatized this third assignment, and the invention of the electronic horn has done the rest. By the time the United States was in the Second World War, it was impossible at times to know who was sitting under the big black cape, for the Presidential car looked like a float advertising an old Cagney or Edward G. Robinson movie.

So the hard experience of American history has compelled the government to act as if half the citizenry were waiting for the chance to take a flyer at any President who dares to come out for air. But this extreme apprehension doesn't explain the police escort for a Senator or a visiting sheik catching a boat. Or a movie star off to dance the Momba. No, indeed. Secrecy, the protection of the 'person', have nothing to do with these rituals, except in so far as the person under convoy is being flattered to think that he is worth assassinating. And here we come to the real point about the police escort: it is a visible and audible mark of privilege. And since the Constitution forbids Americans now and for evermore to make distinctions of rank between themselves, it is only natural that they should look around for little ways of signifying that though they all may be equal, some people – as George Orwell said – are more equal than others. Private beaches by the ocean; the membership of exclusive country clubs; the extreme choosiness of college fraternities and their debased feline opposites, sororities; restrictive covenants on the leasing of houses and apartments: these are all ways of getting above and beyond the humbling brotherhood of man.

There are some less determined and more harmless devices to achieve the same end. A favourite one is to try and wangle, at the end of every year, a motor-car licence-plate that carries a very low number. If your licence number is – as mine is – 4T34-30, you're just another citizen. But suppose it were simply AC 1. Then I would be scrutinized by passing drivers, by pretty women, especially, darn it, and back on the wind occasionally would float the lovely tribute – 'must be a big shot'.

What a triumph of prestige, of what the boys in the eighteenth century called 'singularity', would it be if you could occasionally land a police escort. I knew an Englishman who fixed on this as his consuming American ambition. One way or another he made it and rode with the uniformed

128

dervishes all the way to the docks to meet his cousin, another Englishman who – oh, happy day – wrote English gangster stories. After that the ambitious Englishman had nothing left to fight for, just seemed to pine away. He had conquered the privileges of the brave new world and the last I heard of him he was collecting antiques in Cornwall.

Which brings me irresistibly to the memory of another Englishman who started out with a police escort as a joke and ended with the right to call one any time for the rest of his life that he found himself in West Texas. His story is a modern variation on a classic theme of the English in America. The English dude or dandy was a favourite character in the songs and yarns that came out of the nineteenth-century cattle kingdom. The son of an earl goes West, is given a lot of outrageous poker-face advice, is gravely fitted out by the natives in silk-lined chaps and a pearl-handled revolver and set on the toughest nag in town. The story always goes that the town was struck low with wonder when he bucked through the air with the greatest of ease, stayed firmly on the horse and dismounted to polish his monocle.

My modern variation starts during the last war, when a big, handsome and rather intellectual Englishman arrived in this country on a mission for the British government. Acting on the assumption – which is now, I am told, universal in Britain – that America was here to stay, he conscientiously believed he ought to 'get the feel of the country'. To this end I planned a trip out West for him and arranged for him to spend a couple of days with a great friend of mine in the Davis Mountains, the southern foothills of the Rockies in West Texas. My friend was an irrepressible character, the district attorney of Brewster County, which is about the area of Wales. It is true that in line of duty he had once had to drive a couple of hundred miles to dispose of the rumour of cattle-rustling. But most of the time he was adjudicating land claims, booking men who pulled a gun in a bar-room shindig, paying off small traffic fines for frightened Mexicans. Yet when I wrote and told him to be good to the Englishman he wired back – 'Will give him the works'. My friend, you will gather, was a card. And the old Texan reflex to the visiting

English went into high gear. The Englishman got off the train and my friend left his coat at home just to get into the mood of the thing. He strapped a gun around his impressive middle, rocked on his arches and said, 'Howdy, stranger!' He fed the Englishman the classic meal of bacon and beans, perhaps to remind him of that other hunger which Robert W. Service in a heart-breaking couplet makes practically compulsory on all decent-minded men more than a mile or so from Mother:

Hunger not of the belly kind, that's banished with bacon and beans,
But the gnawing hunger of lonely men for a home and all that it means.

The Englishman was seen to bed and bravely told not to worry overmuch about the coyotes coming down from the hills. 'We have window-screens,' said the host; 'you'll be okay.'

Next morning my friend confided in a bored sort of way that he had to go and 'git' some rustlers a hundred miles or so south, down in the St Helena canyon on the Mexican border. If the Englishman would care to go along for the ride, and wouldn't be too put out by any – er, trouble, he'd be very welcome. He was thrilled. 'I should like it very much indeed,' he said. My crazy Texan had tipped off a brace of state troopers – highway cops – and cued them on when and how to indulge some further nonsense. The little cavalcade whined out of town and the troopers screamed ahead on their motor-cycles, sounding their sirens through the sagebrush for the benefit of nobody but bouncing jack rabbits and a few startled white-tailed deer. At a pre-arranged signal, my friend – who had from now on better be called the D.A. – jammed on his brakes and brought the car to a squealing halt. 'Sorry, pardner,' he yawned and pulled out a slew of rifles from the luggage-carrier and he and the cops started banging away at the horizon. They shouted over their shoulders they were just keeping their hands in. They shot at beer-bottles planted at forty yards on the tops of barrel cactuses. They missed, but the gunfire was immense.

The Englishman came to and squirmed awhile and then

130

wondered, in a reeking interval of the bombardment, if he might, as he put it, 'have a go'.

'Why sure,' they said and tossed him a rifle, as you would hand a surf-fishing rod to a three-year-old. They stuck up bottles at fifty yards. Primly the Englishman raised the rifle to his shoulder. There was a howl and clatter of glass. They moved the target to sixty yards, to seventy, to eighty. He fired again, and again, and again, until the desert was a tinkling cymbal.

The D.A. and the cops have hardly recovered to this day. But in shame, and in some awe, they sirened him home, and put on new uniforms to take him to his train. They told him that any time he came back in the next forty years they had sworn to be his personal bodyguard, complete with siren. From then on, anything he cared to say about English strawberries, the British Empire, the superiority of heatless houses or English shoes – it was gospel, all gospel. My friend this time put his coat on and left his pistol home.

I heard all this from the D.A. himself and when I got back to New York I checked with the Englishman. The facts were as I have related them. When I recalled his astonishing prowess, a pained blush crept up to his forehead. He was a modest man. 'Yes,' he said hesitantly, 'but you know – they really weren't *awfully* good.' It seems he had been on his school team – eight, is it? – the year it won the Ashburton Shield at Bisley.

WILL ROGERS

America, as you know, is a great place for anniversaries and there is hardly a week in the year that some Mayor or Governor doesn't dedicate to a worthy cause or a cause that would like to be thought worthy. So we have National Dog Week, National Shoe Week, National Friendship Week, National Tea Week. Almost nobody but dog-lovers, shoe salesmen and tea-drinkers ever know when these things are going on or what they are about. (Friendship Week has me stumped completely.) Like Mother's Day, no man would dare to say a word against them in public or a good word for them in private. They are tolerated as necessary nuisances, since they do somebody – the florists' associations and the telegraph companies usually – a lot of good. Even children, if they are well brought up, get to take these things with the proper cynicism. The pity is that many good anniversaries pass by unhonoured because it's assumed that some local chamber of commerce thought them up.

A national memorial week has just been proclaimed for a man whose plane crashed in Alaska fourteen years ago, but there's no doubt that if he'd lived, the 4th of November 1949 would have seen a national day of thanksgiving unlike anything that can be imagined outside the resurrection of Mark Twain or Abraham Lincoln. On the 4th of November, we should have had the seventieth birthday of possibly the most endearing American of his time: Will Rogers.

He was a legend in his lifetime and I will try and give you enough of his own words, his own undeceived and yet tolerant humour, to suggest why he was one.

If a Russian or a Finn asked you today who was this Will Rogers, what did he do, you'd have a hard time answering him. A cowboy – yes, that's how he started life, getting nowhere at school and running away and staking his horse outside some Western town every night till he managed to get a job trailing herd from Oklahoma up to Kansas. A world traveller? – well, yes, I suppose so. He heard that the Argentine was good ranching country and hit the road for New Orleans to take a boat. No boats from here, they said, better go to New York. So – with that remarkable ease of roaming that poor American boys seemed to have in the days when they were restricted to a cow pony, a pair of bandy legs, and their wits – he rode and bummed his way to New York. Last boat for Buenos Aires just left, they said, why not go to England? – they appreciate South America, they have boats all the time. So he didn't think twice, but signed on as night-watchman to a shipload of sheep and landed up in London, where he sailed for Rio. And in the same casual way, but sweating it out along with the crew or the cattle all the way, he went to India and South Africa. He broke in horses for the British Army in the Boer War and it might well be one of the forgotten meetings of history that he broke in a charger for Winston Churchill. Then, in the same spirit, to Australia and New Zealand and back to America, all before he was twenty-five.

Still, a generation of cowboys with happy feet have done all this and died obscure. Was he a vaudeville actor? – yes, indeed. He got to showing off rope tricks at county fairs and one night found himself on a stage in Johannesburg roping a dashing horse and lassoing the trombone player. He got into Wild West Shows and ended up in the Ziegfeld Follies, and at state banquets – the favourite performer of Presidents and Kings. Just standing there twirling a rope and saying whatever was on his mind that he'd read in the newspapers that day. This was an idea that came to him years after his talent was known as that of one of the best ropers alive. He felt nervous once before his big trick – roping a steer with one hand and its rider with the other – and he happened to say, 'If this thing comes off, it'll be quite a trick. If it doesn't, you better all go home.' The house roared and this simple and astonished cowboy, part Cherokee Indian, born on Indian territory, was urged by his pals to talk when he felt like it. He did this in New York, in Berlin, in London, in San Francisco, and there has never been an act like him.

Imagine him, small and wiry, hair like soft rope, a nose like a carrot, two quizzical blue eyes with pin-point pupils, two clefts in tanned cheeks, and a huge firm mouth, trembling somewhere between mischief and tears. Imagine him, standing in chaps and shirt before President Wilson or King George V, his right hand doing marvellous things, and drawling observations about taxes, submarines, the Russians, the wonders of Paris. Then he looks up with the calculated shyness that was his protection against humans in the raw, quiets his rope and clears his throat. It's absurd, almost an insult to the whole idea of staged entertainment. A cowboy rambling on before half the hushed statesmen of Europe. 'Your Majesty,' he says, 'you sure put on some great sights in London. But I wish you'd have been with me on Saturday nights in Claremore, Oklahoma. Saturday night was the real thing there. You'd have been crazy about it. Course, ropin' and ridin' and tent shows and circuses is nice stuff. But Saturdays we used to go down to the barber shop *and watch haircuts*!'

He went to the Test Match at Lord's and thought cricket was fine but the lunch and tea intervals made him restless. Asked by the Prince of Wales if the game could ever take in America, he thought it might, with one improvement. And what was that? 'Before the game starts,' he said with a melancholy look, 'I'd line the teams up and say, "Now, listen, fellas, no food till you're through."'

He talked like this all the time, only the pin-points of his eyes glinting in a homely, sad face. His voice had the twanging, syncopated drawl of the Texas panhandle and Oklahoma. He never went beyond the fourth grade at school. And he was one of the few self-made men who truly regretted it. Yet he had a God-given gift for sentences of pure running wit that made hard ideas look as smooth and beautiful as rocks under a trout stream:

'A holding company is the people you give your money to while you're being searched.'

'One revolution is just like one cocktail, it just gets you organized for the next.'

'A difference of opinion is what makes horse-racing and missionaries.'

'Russia is a country that buries its troubles. Your criticism is your epitaph. You simply say your say and then you are through.'

Will Rogers was already a national institution when *The New York Times* had the brilliant idea of asking him to write a daily piece – two sentences or twenty – about the state of the nation. For thirteen years he always appeared in a little box on the front page. And usually two or three sentences were enough, for though he honestly regarded himself as illiterate, his character and mind had long ago done all the work that more learned, but less wise, men have to do on paper before they can say what they would really like to mean.

Will Rogers enjoyed a licence, which was given to no President, to bawl out the army, the taxpayer, the banks, the Presidency itself. And when he said, 'I never met a man I didn't like,' his good nature or self-defence was getting the better of his memory. His great sweetness and unpretending face helped him put over on the American people more unpleasant home-truths than they would have tolerated from a smart man, a handsome man, or a Congressman.

Here are some random bits: 'You know those rascals in Russia along with all their cuckoo stuff have got some mighty good ideas. If just part of 'em work they are going to be hard to get along with. Just think of everybody in a country going to work ... we have just gone along and lived off our country and are lousy with satisfaction of ourselves. Just think what we could do over here if we all worked. Don't get scared, I am not putting this in as a plan.' And this: 'One of my broadminded newspapers wired me, didn't use your article today because you attacked credit and loan. Well, credit means interest and I will attack interest because interest attacks me and you ... Depression ain't nothing but old man interest just gnawing away at us.'

Three days before the election of 1932 he was disgusted with the long summer of election speeches. He told off Mr Roosevelt and Mr Hoover in these words: 'The high office of the President of the United States has degenerated into two ordinarily fine men being goaded on by their political leeches into saying things that if they were in their right minds they wouldn't think of saying. Imagine Mr Hoover last night – "Any change of policies will bring disaster to every fireside in America." Of all the conceit. This country is a thousand times bigger than any two men in it. So you two boys just get the weight of the world off your shoulders and go fishing ... Then come back next Wednesday and we'll let you know which one is the lesser of the two evils of you.'

I suppose men will gravel their brains for a long time to say what is the secret of men like Mark Twain and Will Rogers. Horse sense, common sense, is a first dull stab at a quality which is an almost frightful gift, in people without a smitch of ill-will, of seeing how simply and ruthlessly the world turns. Will Rogers knew more about foreign policy than anyone I know at the United Nations, the fundamental way it works, the uncomfortable plain facts that irritate the professional diplomat but which cannot be explained away. He summed up what three generations of Frenchmen have said at great length when he wrote: 'When you start telling France something about Germany ... it can't be done. France will say, "That's fine from an American angle, but we live across the river from 'em and we know what's going to happen as soon as they're able again. What are you trying to do, shorten our lives?"' And on imperialism: 'This patriotic business is always the Big Brother is helping the Weak Sister. But I don't care how poor and inefficient little Weak Sister is, they like to run their own businesses. Sure, Japan and America and England can run countries perhaps better than China or Korea or India or the Philippines but that don't mean they ought to ... I know men that would make my wife a better husband, but darn it, I'm not going to give her to 'em.'

Looking at the Abyssinian war and the rise of Hitler he wrote sadly and briefly, 'As I see it, little nations has no business being little' and 'Statesmen think they make history; but history makes itself and drags the statesmen along.'

Many of these sound like fighting, even bitter, words. And so they are. Will Rogers would not be the first American to be worshipped for a myth based on a gentle exterior. Most

Americans had to think of him as a kindly sentimentalist in the best of all possible worlds, because he opened up the grave beneath their feet, and if they had dared to take him seriously they would have had to lynch him. But when the molasses starts to flow over his grave, as it will for many years to come, it will be well to remember the honourable core of him, who met many men he despised, and many pretensions he exploded; who lived by compassion and friendliness, out of sheer desperation at the evil things his eyes and his honesty showed him.

THE CASE OF
THE NOVEMBER SUN-TAN

It has been said for many, many years that you will see more pretty girls, even beautiful girls, in New York in a day than you can see anywhere else in a month. I always doubt this until I leave New York for any length of time, when it becomes obvious that it is nothing less than the truth, with a possible doubt being scored in favour of Dallas, Texas. Anyway, it is true enough to take for granted. And I suppose the male New Yorker finds himself in time in the sad case of a professional champagne-taster who gets in his old age, I'm told, to be a beer addict. I know a man, a Southerner, who has never quite reconciled himself to forfeiting the pleasures of the chase, to the excitement of discovering in a mass of people like you and me a really beautiful woman. He has lived in New York so long that he has forced himself to become a connoisseur in reverse. And he goes from party to party looking for plain Jane. I remember the predatory blush that came over his face once when, in a packed room, he spotted an astonishingly homely woman in a corner and gravitated towards her with the delighted cry: 'Now there is a really plain woman.'

To anybody who had knocked around New York for a decade or more, there appeared in the late fall and early winter of 1948 a strange new kind of pretty girl. Her figure, even by American standards, invited the long, low whistle of the snow-bound wolf. She had a rather baffling sun-tan. And her main ambition in life was to carry a big hatbox.

After a brief trip to the United States in the disguise of Basil Rathbone, Sherlock Holmes (who had been doing a little atomic sleuthing at the invitation of Mr J. Edgar Hoover*) guessed at once, in his penetrating way, where she came from, what she was doing here, and on his return to

* The upshot was, of course, the celebrated Fuchs case.

London instructed Watson to buy up some stock in American television.

'But, Holmes,' Dr Watson spluttered, 'what possible connection can a girl with a sun-tan have with – and what's this nonsense about a hatbox? Surely there is nothing remarkable in a healthy girl carrying a hat on the streets of New York.'

Holmes extended himself luxuriously on the sofa and calmly replied, 'The only difficulty, my dear Watson, is that in that hatbox she is not carrying a hat, and her sun-tan has little, if anything, to do with her health.'

'I still maintain, Holmes,' Watson persisted, 'that in that large and notably cosmopolitan city a sunburned girl with a hatbox is hardly a curiosity.'

'On the contrary, Watson,' Holmes said with the irritating calm that so often preceded an apparently preposterous theory, 'she would not be there at all had not the late Sir Herbert Beerbohm Tree once taken a passing interest in the mountain dialect of the State of Pennsylvania.'

Only a long and frequently humiliating experience of his old friend's unpredictable mental vagaries prevented Watson's bursting out in protest. Holmes wheezed meditatively on his pipe. And Watson waited for him to begin.

'During the First World War, Sir Herbert undertook what was to be the last of his tours of the United States. His company was wholly English, but one day a very young man, an American, delivered to him a letter that had been entrusted to a messenger service. The young man had to wait so long for Sir Herbert, and stood so conscientiously in a spot backstage to which a harassed stage manager had assigned him, that he was unwittingly supposed to be a candidate for employment in a crowd scene. The stage manager told him after an hour or so that he had been accepted for a position as a spear-carrier. The young man was quite taken aback, but he had theatrical ambitions of a lowly sort and he allowed the mistake to stand. Eventually he managed to deliver the letter to Sir Herbert, who was fascinated by a certain falling inflection in the young man's speech and his frequent use of dialect phrases that had hitherto escaped the alert ear of Sir Herbert.

He learned that these idiosyncrasies of speech were indigenous to the part of Pennsylvania from which the young man came. Sir Herbert was so delighted with these speech-forms that he insisted the young man be signed on for the whole tour. Now this was a youth possessing in marked degree the American capacity for improving himself at every turn and the native ability to make two dollars appear where formerly there had been only one.'

'How very remarkable!' said Watson.

'So diligent was the young man in his spear-carrying, and so courteous and helpful in his dealings with all the members of the company, that he was soon promoted to be assistant business manager, and at last became stage manager. Suffice it to say that by the time Sir Herbert and his company returned to London, this young man had providently put aside a little cache of money and began to consider branching out into an independent business.'

'You mean he was ambitious to become an actor-manager in his own right?'

'By no means. He might perhaps have gone on to emulate the histrionic triumphs of Sir Herbert, had he not, by a disturbing trick of fate with which, my dear Watson, I am sure you are all too familiar, been diverted by a female.'

'Ah,' said Watson, who was now warming to a conspiracy, 'an adventuress?'

'If you care to put it that way, Watson, I suppose you have the advantage of me. I meant simply that he fell in love. The young woman was distressingly practical and correctly foresaw that her fiancé's merits as a spear-carrier might not necessarily ripen into the career of a Barrymore or a Beerbohm Tree. She suggested that he might do better to acquire, in the vulgar phrase, a steady job. He was reluctant to forgo the world of make-believe, and he sensibly recognized that his talents lay in the direction of commerce. He happened to have a slight acquaintance with a beautiful actress who also had consented from time to time to pose for fashion photographs. She was the lovely Dolores Costello, who subsequently, you may recall, subjected the eminent John Barrymore to a rather prolonged chaperonage from her astute mother.'

'Oh yes, the case of the yachting honeymoon?'

'Correct. This young man idly wondered one day how the couturiers and the manufacturers of women's clothes managed to procure the "models" they needed. He found out that there was no such thing as a professional go-between, who could manage all the tiresome details of arranging photographic interviews at the convenience of the photographer, the manufacturer and the model. He resolved there and then to establish such an institution. He rented a telephone and urged a few personable young women, not the least of whom was Miss Costello, to adopt the extraordinary profession of "modelling", as it came to be called.'

'How very ingenious! What was the name of this enterprising young man?'

'Powers. John Robert Powers. Suffice it to say that within ten years – by the mid-nineteen-thirties – the model agency, as he whimsically described it, had been imitated in many of the world's capitals, although it remains the most celebrated of its kind. The mark of a Powers girl was that she was exceedingly pretty and attracted passers-by on that account alone. But four other peculiarities revealed her to the trained observer – oblige me by not interrupting, Watson – as an employee of Mr Powers's bureau. First, she wore no hat, but had her hair dressed in the style that was *about* to come into fashion.'

'I should have thought,' Watson protested, 'that she would have worn her hair in the height of fashion.'

'I feared you would, Watson. But the incoming fashion is the fashion that no other women have yet been bold or ridiculous enough to adopt. I repeat, therefore, that she wore her hair in the style about to come into fashion, for the simple reason that photographic models are busy being photographed in styles that will appear in the magazines between three and six months from now. This requirement alone caused the second characteristic: that she frequently carried in her hand a small handkerchief and dabbed her nose, which was suffering from a common cold, acquired in the unnatural

141

daily routine of wearing fur coats in midsummer and bathing-costumes in the dead of winter.'

'How extraordinary!'

Holmes impatiently waved his meerschaum and continued:

'The third characteristic was that she was usually in a hurry, in direct proportion to her prettiness, since she might suddenly be called by three or four or more advertisers in the course of a single morning and would have to hasten from one photographic studio to another to fulfil what the Americans call her "assignments", which I beg of you, Watson, not to confuse with assignations.'

'And the fourth characteristic, Holmes?'

'The fourth and most obvious characteristic was that she carried a hatbox.'

'But you said just now that she was hatless.'

'Precisely. She wore no hat because if she were in the business of modelling hats, they would be provided by the hat designer. She might also have to rearrange her coiffure at each assignment, to fit the various roles she was called upon to play.'

'Then why in Heaven's name did she carry a hatbox?'

'She carried a hatbox for the reason that a Coldstream Guards officer wears a bearskin, which I need hardly tell you is not because he any longer wishes to be mistaken for a Fuzzy-Wuzzy in combat. A hatbox was her war-paint, the badge of her tribe, a witness as unmistakable as the black habit of a nun, which testified that she had, on the contrary, embraced the fascinating calling of a model.'

'But, Holmes, what was *in* the hatbox?'

'Ah,' said Holmes with a faint smile, 'that is a problem that has never been conclusively solved. It would be indelicate to probe too deeply into it. Let us charitably say, Watson, that if she carried anything in it at all, you might expect to find lipstick, paper tissues, face powder, a favourite pair of comfortable shoes and all those other impossible oddities without which women maintain they would feel naked, betrayed and temporarily *non compos mentis*.'

'Dear me,' said Watson. 'But I fail to see what connection this young woman can have with your pressing desire to invest in television stock.'

Holmes sighed.

'This young woman was not what prompted me to that shrewd, and I hope profitable, decision. The creatures that baffled you so visibly possessed two additional characteristics.'

'The sun-tan?'

'Quite right.'

'But, Holmes, that is not remarkable in the semi-tropical climate of New York.'

'Indeed, Watson, you could not be more in error. It is unremarkable from the end of May until the beginning of October, when matrons who are comfortably off, and young girls who are pretty enough to be much in demand, have just returned to town from a summer of long weekends reclining in the sun of Long Island, Cape Cod, or the Connecticut or Jersey shores. But at the end of November there has to be another explanation.'

'They have just returned then from Florida?'

'The Florida season is hardly under way. The summer beachcombers have at that season lost their summer sheen and declined, in fact, into a pale yellow jaundice which is, indeed, a very simple index to their income. No, Watson, allow me to cut a long story short. Until this very year, my dear Watson, it was the ambition of comely and energetic young women in the employment of Mr Powers to appear so often and so conspicuously in the public prints that they would attract the attention of a Hollywood motion-picture manager and eventually be rewarded with a film contract. Thereupon they would depart for that outrageous suburb of Los Angeles which Mr Winchell, who you may recall has occasionally given me confidential information, calls Baghdad-on-the-Pacific.'

'But Baghdad, surely, Holmes, is in Iraq?'

'Baghdad-on-the-Pacific is more mundanely known as Hollywood. Now, Watson, your bewilderment will soon be dissipated. We now see hurrying about the streets of New York a type of pretty model who would be indistinguishable from the usual variety of Powers's employee except for the fifth and sixth characteristics that she has a deep sun-tan and is given to wearing rather flashy jewellery.'

'This is unbearable, Holmes. Who is she?'

'She is a Hollywood actress of minor theatrical endowment who, in the slump that the motion-picture industry is fearful about, has been summarily dismissed, has come to New York, and joined a model agency in the hope of making her fame and fortune before the television cameras in New York. Here in the branch of knowledge known as sociology we have a perfect example of what your Aristotle would have called "the reversal of the situation".'

Watson was delighted to discover for the first time that his friend had any acquaintance at all with ancient authors but he replied:

'I don't understand, Holmes, how a situation is reversed when more American girls, who happen to come from the West Coast rather than the East, decide to seek the same mode of employment.'

Holmes's long eyelids closed in pain. He blew eight rings at the gaslight. 'Sometimes, my dear Watson,' he groaned, 'I marvel at the tenacity of your innocence. Aristotle,' he went on acidly, 'said that the reversal of the situation occurs when A does B in order to achieve C but actually achieves D, its opposite. A man marries a woman in order to avoid the fulfilment of the gods' prophecy that he will marry his mother ...'

'Oedipus, of course.'

'The name escapes me. No matter. He marries in haste then, in order to escape the dreadful destiny the gods have allotted to him. However, the woman he marries is, unknown to him, none other than his mother; and the act which he believes to be the act of escape is indeed the act of fulfilment. Similarly, a pretty young woman A joins Mr Powers's B, in order to achieve C – a Hollywood contract. But now C – the girl contracted to Hollywood – joins B (Mr Powers) in the hope of attaining D – fame by television in New York. Or the original girl in New York – A – joins Mr Powers – B

– in order to achieve C – Hollywood – and actually achieves its opposite – D – New York television.'

'It's not quite the same thing, Holmes, as marrying one's mother.'

'It is a modern commercial variant of the same process, and any further information you desire about the phenomenon known as television you will henceforth be good enough to seek under the letter R in my file – R for "reversal of the situation". It is a most striking example of the reversal of the American pioneer movement, which even you, my dear Watson, must recall was in the direction, one hundred years ago precisely, of East to West.'

'You are not suggesting,' said Watson, 'that these attractive young females are coming East to dig for gold?'

'I am not suggesting it,' Holmes replied drily, 'because the name gold-digger has already been suggested for them whatever direction they were travelling in. I am, however, suggesting that for the first time in the most astonishing century of American history, a noticeably talented, or perhaps I should say well-endowed, group of young American women are seeking their fortunes east of the Rocky Mountains, in the place their grandparents started from.'

'You foresee, then, Holmes, the decline of the West?'

Holmes thought hard for fifteen or twenty minutes, shivered slightly in his dressing-gown and replied:

'I foresee, rather, that the wheel is about to come full circle. The crude little photographic studio in New York City, where Miss Mary Pickford first enacted a motion-picture part – *The New York Hat* was, I think, the name of the photoplay – was thought of at the time as a stepping-stone to motion-picture fame on the distant shores of the Pacific. It is now the Mecca of young women who have lived surrounded by that fame.'

Watson protested long and loud at this: it was inconceivable that Hollywood, which had become the world capital of movie entertainment, could be facing a serious decline. Holmes pooh-poohed this argument and delivered himself of this final little homily:

'I am afraid, Watson, that you share a delusion about the

metropolitan stature of Hollywood which is common to those
who have never been there, and those who have never been
anywhere else. Hollywood is a suburb of the old Spanish city
of Los Angeles, to which some indeed have denied the name
of city. It has been better called, "Twenty-four suburbs in
search of a city". One of these is the district of Hollywood,
lying on the foothill slopes of the Santa Monica mountains.
So obscure is this community in the eyes of the American
government that only this year, 1948, was Hollywood granted
its first post-office. Contrary to the popular belief, Hollywood
has almost no film studios. They are all in other districts,
notably in Culver City, Burbank and West Los Angeles. The
only street in Hollywood known to history is a road through
the mountains, the Cahuenga Pass, through which passed
the famous expeditions of Portola and De Anza. Until 1853
Hollywood had no houses at all, and the first one was made –
significantly – of mud. As late as 1896 the most dramatic
event that happened there was the daily arrival of the stage
coach. By 1910 it was a small village of farmers, Methodists,
estate agents, and especially of shepherds. It was a sheep-town.
I believe that only recently a local law was established which
specified how many sheep you were allowed to drive at high
noon along the streets.'

Watson was, as so many Americans have said of him, fit
to be tied.

'But Heavens, Holmes,' he cried, 'you surely can't ignore
the fabulous history of the nineteen-twenties and thirties,
when the population went up to something like a quarter of a
million?'

Holmes waved an irritated, bony hand.

'Mere vulgar panic, Watson,' he declared. 'All those people
were blindly seeking the twentieth-century medium of entertainment. They thought they had found it in the motion
picture. History will record, my dear Watson, they made the
false start in the direction of television.'

'Humph,' growled Watson. 'It looks, then, as if Hollywood
would fulfil the fate which that editor in Kansas – C. P. Scott,
wasn't it? – called the typical American destiny – from shirt-
sleeves to shirtsleeves in three generations.'

The fog in Baker Street was now so dense that it swirled in through the blinds. Holmes gave a loud, horrifying cough and clutched his chest.

'No, Watson,' he replied, 'from sheep-town to sheep-town in two generations.'

MOVING A HOME

There was a time when New Yorkers moved their homes every 1st of October. They did it from choice, just as long as there was a choice of other apartments in other parts of town. The most incurable New Yorker I know, who wouldn't think of living anywhere else, would have thought he was sinking into dotage and arthritis if he had not gone tramping around town every July picking out another nest, another home, another place to be happy in. In those days, which were not so long ago, a real-estate agent was a different breed of cat. He was solicitous and friendly and paced you on your tour of inspection with the dog-like devotion of a trainer jogging alongside the world's heavyweight champion. This species has died out: a real-estate agent is now a go-between who stays by a telephone, snarls at people who want to change their neighbourhood (they are Communists, most likely), and, just before he hangs up, remembers a vacant place on a traffic-jammed crosstown street which he will let you have as a special favour if you'll deposit a thousand dollars for goodwill or buy the apartment. This deal is known as a 'co-operative apartment'. You agree to co-operate with the owner of the building by paying the maintenance on the apartments that may be abandoned in hard times.

For several years, ever since the war ended, I had hoped to meet up again with an old-style renting agent. I knew one agent, a cordial brisk lady who had once rented me an apartment in a handsome building overlooking Central Park. Three or four times a year I would phone her and ask for anything she had. A ripple of bawdy laughter would come over the phone. One day a year ago she rang me. She had something for me. I was uptown in a flash. We met in the lobby of the building and she led me up to the fourth floor. There is a ritual understanding between agent and what they call intending tenant not to talk about money matters in

148

public places. So we waited till we got inside the privacy of the apartment. Unfortunately, the windows were open, and it was then I saw that the place fronted on a crosstown street, which once had a little stimulating traffic: an occasional bus, a cab sliding by, a doctor starting up his car at the sidewalk after a hurried call. Now, there are fleets of buses (just more people alive, I guess). The most law-abiding people have stopped paying the insane rates asked for garage rent and there is double-parking on both sides of the street, triple-parking in the rush hours. The apartment was blue with New York's famous ozone, otherwise known as carbon monoxide. The agent and I started to shout at each other the relevant commercial details. I gathered that I could have this corner of Babel for my very own on deposit of ten thousand dollars as 'compensation' to the outgoing tenant, who had 'done the place over' at his own expense. He had converted a bedroom into a dining-room, and a dining-room into a third bathroom, and generally messed up the compact original plan. After shelling out this tribute, I would be allowed to pay an impressively heavy rent each month for the privilege of living there. I went back to our little hole-in-the-wall on 71st Street and resigned myself to a tenement existence.

For years we had hemmed and hawed about the inadequacies of our home. But from necessity we had got to look on it affectionately, an old comfortable shoe of a kind that they don't make any more. For one thing it didn't look like a New York apartment. It looked like the top floor of a rambling house in San Francisco, with irregular bays and windows that bulged, and floors that sagged slightly, making odd curves in the rooms. A living-room you could draw heavy partitions across. A corridor as long and clattery as a bowling alley. And a little dining-room at the end of it, so far away we used to say let's go to 70th Street and eat. It was rundown and seedy and inefficient – a little oasis of old-world incompetence in the middle of plunging skyscrapers and penthouses and bedrooms across the way throbbing with air-conditioning machines. We had, for instance, a bright naked bulb that hung right over one bathtub from an open strand of wire. And there were times when I expected to hear

149

somebody splashing away in the bosom of my family suddenly let out a yell and be clutched to the bosom of the Lord.

How was it different from a typical American apartment?
Well, the main thing about the design of American homes
these many decades is the absence of doors. You come in
and 'Why, hello!' everybody screams, because everybody can
see you. There, on the right, is the living-room framed in a
big opening, and across from it, framed in another big
opening, is the dining-room. They do have doors on the
bedrooms and bathrooms, but everything else is constructed
on what the modern architects call the 'open' or 'free-flowing'
plan. (I'll bet the man who thought up this style was a bachelor.
The 'open' plan is a fatal invitation to have children free-
flowing through the place at every hour of the night and day.)
Don't misunderstand me. The modern boys have simply
appropriated for their own and expanded a plan that is seventy
or eighty years old. To have doors on all the rooms of your
house, you'd have to have the eccentricity or the money
to buy an old Revolutionary House, something at any rate
not much later than about 1820. For some reason or other
Americans don't like two normal features of the European
house. They don't care for doors and they don't like ceiling
lights. So they also have the ceilings smooth and insist that
each room shall have lots of what you call points and we
call outlets. Four lamps in a living-room is about the minimum, eight or ten is not unusual.

The door-allergy has a sound practical cause. It is the
stubborn belief of Britons that Americans invented what they
call steam heat, and you call central heating, sometime in the
nineteen-twenties or thirties. But like many other American
gadgets, which are not gadgets at all, but examples of the
calm American genius for applying intelligence to daily life,
central heating came in in a rudimentary form as long ago
as the eighteenth century. They learned by then to cast off their
English fatalism. They saw no reason to submit without a
protest to whatever climate God ordained outside. They put
wood-burning furnaces in their cellars and let the heat come
up through grills in the floor of all the rooms. By the time
they had switched from wood to coal and coal to oil, there

was no sense in having doors, which from their point of view could now be looked on as a crude device to keep the people in any one room warm by keeping the cold air out. The temperature in the hall, the bedroom, the dining-room, the bathroom, could be the same. If you wanted it cool in your bedroom, or if you were an Anglo-Saxon and insisted on trembling in your morning bath, well, you could simply shut the grill. This is the principle on which is based the later refinement of thermostats in the main rooms which respond to a finger's touch, set the furnace roaring until the temperature is precisely what you asked for, at the hour you set on the accompanying alarm clock. Modern American architects are already beginning to abandon this system as a clumsy Colonial relic. 'Radiant heat' is the thing. And they mean in the next few years to bottle up in your house the heat from the sun and tap the bottle when they need it.

But this is far from the humble amenities of our chicken-coop on 71st Street. Englishmen liked this place, because they don't as a rule like to sit and read in a big open room, with a big black space between them and the front door or another dim-lit room. You are, let's face it, cantankerous. Americans put it another way, and say Englishmen suffer from agoraphobia and just don't feel snug unless they are shut in.

Well, our old apartment – I think the building went up in the Stone Age, sometime around 1900 – bent and sloped all over the place. It was endearing in other ways. Every bedroom had a washbasin and wall-cupboards built in. They stopped doing this about 1918, when the custom developed of having a bathroom for every three rooms, and in upper-middle-class homes a bathroom for every one or two bedrooms. Ours was an ancient house all right, but even we, with four bedrooms, had two bathrooms. And few American houses, however quaint, are ancient enough to require the colossal stupidity of a wardrobe. Closets, with doors, are another simple and obvious blessing that Americans introduced into their homes something between a hundred-and-fifty to two hundred years ago.

But, what with the cracking plaster – we had a whole

sagging rhomboid in our bedroom ceiling, so that you never knew if you'd wake up successfully or not – you can see how life was a hazard at the best of times. The place was so broken down when I first saw it – my wife was living there alone with her children as a war widow – that I had an uprush of chivalry and I shouted to her, 'Marry me, and let me take you away from all this!' You know what the war did to chivalry and housing. After the ceremony I moved in with her as a legal boarder. Just me and my naked body. All my books, pictures, pen-knives, love-letters, cameras, films and old bills had to go into storage, on which – being no business man – I paid eight dollars a month for seven years.

In 1949 came, in the course of wedded bliss, Susie. And what with her waking up her devoted brother and his crying, 'Get that brat out of here', Susie came to sleep in the anachronism known as a dining-room. I won't go into all the distressing circumstances that made us crave to move into more space, where these Letters wouldn't have to be plotted with a diaper pin between my teeth. One great day came an unsolicited phone call from a real-estate agent with the dizzy news that what we wanted was now, after six fruitless years, available. It was high up on Fifth Avenue and overlooked the park. We bit and set the date, the 2nd of December as I easily recall, because Mr Attlee, the Prime Minister of Great Britain, heard about it, and decided at once to fly to Washington on a matter of peace or war. Just like the convicts on Alcatraz, who heard I had arrived in San Francisco on my honeymoon and obligingly went berserk, with the result that I stayed up till three the first night cabling a story about the siege of Alcatraz. Well, once again a political crisis came to aggravate a crisis in my domestic life. Nothing serious, you understand, just incompatibility, mental cruelty, the prospect of marital chaos.

To any normal wife the point should now be sufficiently clear. My wife would have to do the moving. I would have to move to Washington for Mr Attlee and his crisis. She happens to be a veteran workhorse. And the day before we moved in she walked into the place – which was to our cave-dwelling eyes something like Versailles without the couches –

cleaned the place out, swept and washed it, plastered odd cracks in the living-room walls, sized it, mixed the paints and painted it. Landlords don't do these things any more. Husbands will understand that I did not congratulate my wife on this tremendous chore. She can labour like Hercules. But she doesn't like to feel like Hercules. Anyway, ahead of her was the moving. She resented it. Most of all, she resented Mr Attlee, who saved me from a stiff stretch as a stevedore and plumber's mate. When I came back from Washington five days later, everything was sparkling. Pictures were up, carpets down, rooms painted in many colours (one colour, one room, that is), the kitchenware and cutlery washed and arranged in pantry cupboards and breakfronts. There was a striped bass crackling in a pool of wine and butter. It was wonderful. I walked to the window, and there was Central Park.

Then I felt a little sad and suddenly lonely. Not lonely in the privileged way that great cities let you be. But out of it, an outcast from a community I had hardly been aware of. It was the community bound by 72nd Street and 68th Street on Lexington Avenue. Suddenly we were displaced persons, who knew nobody. Why? Because we had left our neighbourhood. Like all New York neighbourhoods, it was three blocks long. There is nothing known or defined about this fact. It is not a system, like the even-numbering of eastbound and the odd-numbering of westbound streets. But it just happens that almost anywhere you live in New York, everything you ever want is round one corner or the other. Meat, flowers, newspapers, a shoe shine, a picture to hang, a bottle to drink, a plumber, an electrician, a doctor (in case somebody got electrocuted on that bathtub wire), a delicatessen with tamales from Mexico and marmalade from England; an Italian vegetable man, a police phone-box, a mail-box, a baker, watchmaker, a silversmith, three drug-stores, two lunch counters, five restaurants, a movie theatre: the whole of life. All gone, and all the people we knew and cracked a morning smile with. Before we left, I did the rounds. I said well, good-bye, Fred, Tony, Mark, Don, Vincent, Luigi, Abe. 'Too bad,' they said in various ways; 'come and see us sometime.' We were moving a mile uptown. But it would have been the same if we'd gone only four blocks. That would have put us just across the border.

I had read about this characteristic of New York in E. B. White's charming essay on our town. But he didn't move me to feel it, because I'd been too long in one place. Now I realized the triumphant, the touching charm of New York. This great, plunging, dramatic, ferocious, swift and terrible big city is the most folksy and provincial place I have ever lived in. New York is the biggest collection of villages in the world.

Of course we have moved into another village, bounded by Fifth and Madison Avenue. But the villagers, like all villagers, are leery of strangers. I strolled over to Madison Avenue and asked for a pound of tomatoes. The swarthy Italian face looked up, and the eyes smiled. 'To-mah-toes?' he said. 'Fifth Avenya talk, huh?' – and yelled to the back of the store, 'Pounda tomaytas.'

In this simple exchange, I became an acknowledged citizen of the new village.

A BABY IS MISSING

I suppose everybody who ever stops at a news-stand on his way to work has at the back of his mind a very simple distinction between a good newspaper and a bad one, or better, between a 'heavy' newspaper and a 'light' one. It is a curious thing that the heavy newspapers in most countries tend to steer clear of the great human stories in the news, while the light newspapers should be the ones to take an instinctive interest in such profound things as murder, kidnapping, rape and infidelity: for surely the deepest human feelings are involved in such goings-on. The other curiosity is this: the people who write for heavy newspapers are just the people who, on their own confession, pretend to a superior taste in literature. They will brood long and talk strenuously over a murder in Dostoevsky, a pickpocket in Dickens, a spy in Joseph Conrad. But lift the murder or pickpocket out of literature and into Sheffield or Camden Town, and they assume no journalist worth the name would give his talent to such squalid stuff. The result is, it seems to me, that the best stories get badly written up, while the dull abstractions that are the same in all countries and all generations – politics, economics – are treated with solemn care.

Luckily, the United States is not yet blasé enough to keep up this artificial distinction between life and literature. With the result that the most serious newspapers in the country – and there are no better newspapers anywhere than the best three or four American dailies – always have in their active employ a small stable of feature-writers who are very much aware of the teeming life that is going on all around them. By teeming life, I'm not thinking of the special tempo or intensity of life in New York: I mean the daily life of the streets, the markets, the slums, the private joys and grief of anybody from the Mayor of New York to a couple of Puerto Rican immigrants who sleep out nights in an uptown garage.

155

In the spring of 1950 a story broke in New York which here, and only here, swept Germany and Congress, and the risk of war, right off the front pages of all the light and heavy newspapers. It seems to me to be one of the news stories of the century, and I think it's worth telling over to anyone who has ever felt a pang for somebody else's disappointed hopes.

It is a story about a coloured girl, eighteen years of age, and a coloured baby, ten days old.

The first day of spring that year came into New York with a spatter of snowflakes. The night of the 21st of March was no time to be out. It was raw and misty, and even the midnight movies on Broadway were doing poor business. That night a young coloured woman, a Mrs Holden, was taken by her anxious husband to an uptown hospital, the Lincoln Hospital, and delivered of a premature baby. It was put in an incubator right away. It weighed two pounds and a few ounces at birth, and the doctors told the trembling couple they could do no more than their best. Nine days later, the 30th of March, was a wheezing, freezing night. The night nurse of the incubator ward came in to see how the premature babies were doing, peeked at the thermostat, looked around and into the Holden incubator and – the Holden baby was gone. She brought an orderly and a doctor running. But sure enough the baby had vanished. When the parents arrived they were almost crazed, but the doctor had to tell them the pitiful truth: the baby then weighed two pounds, eleven ounces. If it had been taken outside on such a night, it might live for an hour, two hours at most. The parents shuffled off home. The doctor put a tentative stroke across the baby's progress chart. A police siren whined outside and the next morning the tabloids reported a routine kidnapping. The F.B.I. was called in, and that was apparently the end of the story.

Three weeks later, a pleasant housewife who lives way uptown was doing her housework one morning and listening to the radio. And up came that tune again, a pleasant jingle going the rounds of the dancehalls and the disc jockeys. A song called 'Don't Call Me a Nosey Man'. This woman couldn't get the thing out of her head. She decided she would clean up a bit and go out and buy the gramophone record of it. She went to a little store on 125th Street in the heart of Harlem and asked the assistant to play it first. While it was jingling away, a chunky, strutting coloured girl in her teens strolled up and said, 'Oh, I *like* that record.' The housewife turned to look at her and suddenly knew the face. She had seen it once before, weeks ago. She looked again, and she knew it was the face of a girl holding a baby on a cold night. The housewife was sure it was the same girl, but whereas three weeks ago this girl had been a forlorn ignorant mother, she was now in the housewife's eyes a 'person wanted'. The housewife too read the newspapers. Before the girl could say another sentence the housewife dashed from the store and grabbed the nearest cop. He was an old-timer, he'd seen hysterical women before. 'Take it easy, lady,' he said; 'now what's all this about a blanket?' By the time he was up and on the job the teen-age coloured girl was gone. Then a week after that, by a mad coincidence, a little strutting, chunky coloured girl went into a bus depot on 42nd Street. Of all things, she went up to a cop. She wasn't too consecutive in her story. It seemed she'd had some trouble lately in a store in Harlem. The cop motioned to another cop, who came up and said, 'I know that girl; she lives in my hotel.' So she did, a seedy little place way over on the West Side. Well, the cops phoned the station-house and the F.B.I. connected in no time, and the word went out over the police-car radios that a young coloured woman 'wanted' had hopped a bus on 42nd Street, the terminal for buses that serve the South. In fact, the girl had not taken a bus. She had wandered out of the bus station and gone across the street and over to her hotel. But by that time the F.B.I. men were stopping traffic and dredging through bus stations from New York City all the way down to New Orleans.

Next day they found her, in a tiny hotel bedroom. She was married to a porter in the hotel. She wept out her story. She had done nothing wrong. She was unhappy because only lately she'd given birth to stillborn twins. Please would they get out and leave her alone. At last she broke down and said it: she had kidnapped the baby. But the detectives knew as

157

well as she did that the baby was dead. They had cast a roving eye around everything and tapped the tattered wallpaper for hidden panels and looked under this and that. All right, then, sorry, ma'am, they'd have to book her. Too bad about the baby.

They were at her door and on the way out when one of them held up his index-finger. From across the hall came a thin broken wail, like the complaint of a powerful kitten. The cops and detectives jumped across the hall and broke the lock on a small door and pulled the door open. The heat from inside came at them like a ten-pound roast. It was a room no bigger than a linen-closet. And there was the baby.

Now we can go back to the nipping, frosty night of the 30th of March and straighten everything out. The girl, eighteen years old, had, as she said, just had stillborn twins. She was fairly frantic for a baby. And in the active misery of her loss she decided quite straightforwardly to go get one. On the afternoon of the 30th of March she somehow got into the Lincoln Hospital. I said, I think, she had a plump, confident strut. Well, the nurses and doctors thought, if they thought at all, that she was a charwoman, or kitchen worker, or something. She marched around the corridors, took elevators up and down, sallied into this room, this lab, that dispensary, and kept her eyes open. By nightfall, she had the premature-baby section very well located. She went there, walked straight in, unhooked a door, lifted the top of the first incubator she saw and took the baby out – two pounds and eleven ounces. She put it under her coat, took an elevator down and out on to the street. This is where the good Lord and neighbourly sense did more to help her than the split-second timing of a bank robbery.

She walked three blocks to the underground station, went into a rest-room, took off the bright red skirt she had on and wrapped it around the baby. The train came in. The conductor said, 'Lady, that's no way to warm a baby on a night like this. You better go and stop a cab and get a blanket some place.' She went upstairs and out and walked straight into a nearby apartment, and in no time was back with another woman holding a blanket. She thanked the woman, hailed a cab, put the squawling baby on the seat and started to put her red skirt on. The driver was mildly outraged. 'I'm sorry, miss,' he said; 'you can't dress in my cab.' They tossed it back and forth a while, and the cab-driver said, 'Just can't *do* it, ma'am.' But he knew a nice lady who'd let her dress at her place. So he drove her to the home of a friend, the housewife we met with the tune on her mind. There the girl dressed, thanked the housewife, and the taxi-driver drove her downtown to a bus terminal. Somebody who worked around there remembered this bulging sight when, three weeks later, the cops started to ask questions in the same terminal.

None of this answers the aching question: 'How did she possibly keep the baby alive?' When at last it was returned to the hospital, it weighed three pounds, one ounce, a gain of six ounces, and was squealing a little more lustily now. The doctors said – 'a miracle'. An act of God, said another. Well, we all know that God helps them that help themselves. And what had this forlorn, half-crazed, illiterate coloured girl done to nurture this miracle? She had bought a twenty-five-cent book, a reprint about baby care, at a drugstore. She had nosed around a clinic and talked with nurses. And when the detectives broke into the little room, they found some paper-backed books: 'The American Woman's Cook Book'; a Bible; 'The New Modern Home Physician'; two pulp magazines – 'Ideal Love' and 'Love Should be Laughter'. They found a folding carriage lined with an electric blanket. There was an electric grill. By its side a row of baby formulas, and twelve bottles with those sterilized nipples that pop up without touching. A pan of water and sterilizing tweezers. The proper vitamin extracts. Baby powder, absorbent cotton, baby oil. And the essential feeding weapon, for a child that size: an eye-dropper.

At the hospital later an obstetrician, still full of doubt, said, 'But there were two things she *couldn't* know: the atmosphere around a premature that size has to be humid, and must be maintained strictly at 96 degrees.' 'Well,' said a cop who was on the expedition to get her, 'she had a pan of boiling water on the electric grill, steaming the place up

159

like mad. And, oh yes – up against the inside lintel of the door was a thermometer.'

He remembered he had seen it and noted down the temperature. He opened his pad now and turned the pages. It was right there. It had read precisely 96 degrees.

They brought the girl into court about a month or so later. Very reliable psychiatrists had looked her over and simply testified nothing but the truth: she was quite mad, a psychotic. And so, quite rightly, since psychotics are beyond the intelligent handling of life, not to say a threat to you and me, they put her away. The baby is at this writing a year old and very fit and laughing its head off.

MARGARET AND MISSOURI

I don't know any job in journalism that is harder to do than a profile or character sketch of the royal family of a country that is, or has to be, on cordial relations with your own. However well the journalist may know his rulers or their families, he is gagged at the start. Honesty, frankness, a real attempt to be objective, is impossible, because the limits of his curiosity about his subjects are set from the outside. And they are very rigid limits. I'm not thinking of censorship. I'm thinking of something far more binding on the imagination and the spirit of inquiry. I mean courtesy and tact.

There is a further handicap on a broadcaster trying to do this kind of thing, since all broadcasting – whether it is a gardening talk or a battle report – is a form of suspense, in which the listener tolerates the talker because he's not quite sure what's coming next or how it will all turn out. If I tell you I am going to do a character sketch of Mr Truman or Queen Juliana or Mrs Roosevelt, you know at the start how it is going to turn out. They are going to be nice people. There is no other conclusion possible, if international relations are to be preserved. Just as during the war, it would have been equally impossible to do a talk about Dr Goebbels – a very brilliant man, by the way – without having him come out an unmitigated villain.

It has not always been so, and we make a mistake if we think that public reticence about the character of the ruler is an old Anglo-Saxon tradition. It is in fact not much older than the reign of King George V. We have certainly come a long way since the day after the death of George IV, when the London *Times* appeared with black borders and an editorial that began : 'There can hardly be a wet eye in the kingdom for this debauched monarch.'

Now America, as you may have heard, has not had a King for some time. Its President is no more sacred than a Prime

Minister, and he and his family come in for all the kidding and the gibes and the sometimes brutal slander that the lax American libel laws allow. The exact American equivalent of the King of England in this tradition of public respect is no human being. It is the American flag. And no journalist however drunk or ribald, and no public man however indignant, dares to make a joke about the flag or fail to bow before the very elaborate series of observances and customs that Congress embodied in a law. Thus, the flag may never touch the ground except at sundown. It must never be mended if it is torn. It is a punishable act to use the design of the flag for any sort of public or private decoration – a flower-bed, say, or a cushion, or an emblem on a chocolate box. Americans like to think that they are much more honest in their writing about the President and his family than you are about the Royal Family. But this is not a sensible comparison. It is like a Methodist saying he is much more critical of the vicar's wife than a Catholic is of the Pope. They do not represent the same symbol.

Now even though the United States doesn't have a royal family, it does have what we call a First Family. And though Americans of the out-party always call the President's wife laughingly by her first name, some of the same respect in public is shown to the First Lady, as she is called. When Margaret Truman, the First Lady's daughter, went on a holiday to Europe you might think this would be a rather dizzy experience of moving for once in circles which, if they are not exactly new to her, are not her daily round, as they are, for instance, of Britain's Princesses. From all accounts, Margaret conducted herself with the tact and grace and gaiety that we should expect of her. When I say expect of her, I don't mean that we expect her to be on a special kind of behaviour when she goes abroad and meets Presidents and Kings. I mean we expect her to be what any other American girl of her special type was bound to be, wherever she was: herself.

You'll say, there he goes. He starts out like all official biographers by saying he's going to be frank, and in no time he's saying what a happy break it is for the nation that this particular fairy princess is an extraordinary, a charming, a wonderful person ... in her own right. 'In her own right' is the patented trademark of official biographers trying to make their hypocrisy sound like good detective work.

So Margaret Truman, after all, is a nice girl, is she? No, she isn't. And she isn't pretty either. She is a healthy, gay, irrepressible, slangy, madcap girl with a gift of hair-breadth tact. And if anybody alive manages to bully the President, she is the one who does it. Of course, like any other human being, she is a person in her own right, but this can be a very unpleasant discovery. They used to say about an old presidential candidate, who shall be nameless, that 'you have to know him really well in order to dislike him'.

But I wouldn't have chosen to discuss Margaret Truman at all if she wasn't an agreeable person. What I want to say about her is that she is no different from a few million other Western and Midwestern girls; and that what made her a success on her European tour is nothing personal, but an end-product of the society she sprang from – of the free interplay between the farming and city life of the Midwest. One of the true things about the hurly-burly that is roughly and sometimes falsely called the social democracy of this country is the fact that you cannot go into a restaurant or a lunch-counter and tell where a girl was born, or what is her father's income, from the way she uses a knife and fork, or by the dishes she chooses. This is only partly a happy legacy of the American character. It is in the main a gift from God. For the great natural resources of this country, combined with the national foods that each immigrant race insisted on having, have made every truck-driver and city family in America, high or lowly, acquainted at first-hand with all the homeliest dishes of Europe. Every American youth knows what ravioli is, or bortsch, or wiener schnitzel, or strudel, or smorgasbord, or sauerkraut, or goulash, because he has had them. To understand this is to be on the way to understanding the natural poise of Margaret Truman, born to an unemployed farmer in his fortieth year, just gone bankrupt in the haberdashery business, with a farm mortgaged to every acre, and loaded with debt.

There are two points about the Midwest that are worth

noticing here. One is that, unlike many places in the East, the rich (where there *are* any rich) and poor go to school together; and since nobody likes to feel foolish as he is getting into his teens, the majority tends to set the style of manners, dress, social intercourse. They do not set a greatly different standard of speech, though, for in America regional speech as such does not carry a social stigma; and a rich or educated Southerner, a rich or educated Midwesterner, talks like his fellows. He would be some kind of freak if he talked like any kind of New Englander or New Yorker. Now, this characteristic of the Midwest – it is characteristic of all American regions except the biggest cities of New York, New England and the South, which are closer to the bulk of American private schools – means that over a very great area of society manners are much the same. It is an old story, and has a lot to do with the conditions under which this land was broken and a dour and mixed crew of hungry voyagers was made into a nation. Starting in New England, the first Puritans couldn't afford to allow the parson and the teacher and the farmer and carpenter to set their separate ways of life. The bishop had to carry a gun or risk a scalping. The teacher had to be able to build a house or go cold. The first New Englanders had one urgent goal, and it was not of their choosing. It was survival. But the New Englanders who stayed in the East built up a society that became in time fairly well stratified, though still socially looser than any they had left behind. This persisting looseness has irritated several generations of upper-crust Yankees, with the result that snobbery is a whole-time job over here and is therefore more conspicuous and more pathetic than it is with the same people in Britain.

The New Englanders who liked the social freedom of the first settlements moved West. And in a way, the Midwesterner is a more typical old New Englander than the first families of Boston. He has remained a jack-of-all-trades, because he faced – in some places two hundred years later – the same conditions that the Pilgrim Fathers met.

It is always a baffling thing to a continental European to find no peasants in America, and secondly to find that he cannot identify a farmer on sight. The Midwestern farmer is not often a man whose father and grandfather were also farmers. And there is no guarantee that his son will be one, or even that he himself will be one in the next five years. He may take a fling at running a garage, or going into politics, or being an electrician or a builder. The typical Midwest farmer is a phrase on paper and very hard to pin down on the land. He may be a man who lives in a small town and drives his car to his land, where he rents machinery and hires hands and works it himself for no more than six weeks of the year. He may commute from the city to supervise his share-croppers or tenants. He may be a businessman leaving the field work to a foreman (until the foreman quits to become a road supervisor). If he has a big farm and lives on it, he will have a big house too and lots of help. Whatever is his type, he is rarely a man who in the old-world fashion cannot remember any other kind of work, who goes from his cottage to the fields every day of the year. His wife and children, for another thing, don't necessarily work the farm. They will be going to school, hopping around in automobiles, writing mash notes to film stars, picking out a dress from a mail-order catalogue for the high-school dance two weeks from Saturday. Another thing – the Midwest farmer eats a great deal better than the city man – three or four meats come your way, a fricasseed chicken, a raft of vegetables, two or three cheeses, several sweets, gallons of cold milk and hot coffee. But in most other respects his family's ways are city ways. And whereas the banker's son may decide to be a farmer, the farmer's son may go into a bank. There is nothing final about these changes. Harry Truman can do all the chores of a farm, and most of the jobs around an automobile service station. He has been a roadmender, a judge, a haberdasher and a bookworm. And Margaret Truman in her teens, by the time she reached Washington, had rubbed shoulders with a wider span of society than she would have done if her father had been a New York stockbroker or policeman.

In her short life no occupation was mysterious and none likely to inspire awe. It is no accident that she took to the White House as she would have taken with equal zest to a California citrus ranch or a life at Fort Riley as a cavalry officer's daughter. Mr Truman didn't want to be Vice-President, because he suspected, as many people did, that the next man in that job would be President, and Mr Truman said, 'The White House is no place for children.' He belittled the value of a Midwestern farm background and underestimated the adaptability it fosters.

So Margaret Truman happens to be just a Midwestern girl used to moving around and could take in her stride a Washington society in which old farming friends and Kansas City boys juggle drinks with ambassadors and lawyers. If she had been what they call a well-brought-up Eastern girl, I think she would have been more likely to blush and stumble at Buckingham Palace and Versailles. But she knows only one way to behave – the way she has always done. And her manner is easy and spry and ironic, because she came from a very civilizing school – from the farming-city life of the Midwest, where you run into so many skills that ignorance is no shame; where the judge and tractor-hand, the postman and the lawyer had better all be treated with equal respect. They may be switching jobs any day.

THE BIG BRAIN

The second week in March is a grievous time for millions of Americans. The 15th of March is the deadline for the federal income-tax returns. This is a bad time in any country, but no other country has an income-tax form so wordy, niggling and elaborate. This is because the Bureau of Internal Revenue, true to the American prejudice, lets everybody make himself out to be a special case. By this system, no two men, even in the same sort of job, and earning exactly the same salary, will pay the same amount of tax. The harrowing complications set in when you face the page marked 'deductions'. There are certain fairly simple categories. You may deduct all medical expenses that amount to more than five per cent of your gross income. You may deduct contributions to charities. You may deduct the cost of drugs you got on prescription, the taxes you paid to your state last year, interest on mortgages and property taxes, and alimony – which is a major industry in the United States. You may deduct in New York our third and most annoying form of taxation – the city sales tax, which you pay whenever you go into a store to buy anything except food and medicine, literally everything that costs more than ten cents. This alone takes quite a lot of figuring. How often did I go to the movies, or buy a dish-cloth, or a hat, a pair of overshoes for the children, a pencil, a restaurant meal over a dollar?

The Bureau of Internal Revenue and its horde of mathematical drones has lately added insult to injury. They have in several big cities installed electronic calculators – they look like a couple of big trunks open for packing, but are in fact already jammed with hundreds of vacuum tubes. They are the babies of the giant electronic computer – the so-called electronic brain – they have up at Harvard and in a display centre here in New York.

It appears that of the income-tax returns made out and

dutifully posted before midnight of the 15th of March approximately one in four is incorrect. Most of these mistakes it seems are errors made in the simple good faith of bad arithmetic. Some of them indicate a constitutional inability to follow the economic maze of the instructions. Some however amount to cunning attempts to double-cross the income-tax collector. The staff of the Bureau of Internal Revenue is always described as 'huge'. But it is never huge enough. For every income-tax return has to be scrutinized and checked, and amended. And then down the years winds the dreary routine of writing insults, interviewing the taxpayer, checking his personal files of chequebooks, leases and so on. I say down the years, because if by a happy mischance you paid more than you ought to, it's likely to be a year or two before the Bureau can humanly get around to sending you the refund. I was challenged about three years ago on my 1946 income tax – they had just got around to me. When we were through, after a feud conducted with hysteria on my part and phlegm on theirs, it came out that they owed me a hundred and seven dollars. They said they'd send me a cheque. This was a prospect that kept me on edge for about three months. Then I settled into boredom, then a cynical resignation. Two weeks ago, the cheque arrived. However, it was not for a hundred and seven dollars. It was for a hundred and forty. The difference was the amount of interest that had accumulated. Our government of course is a good government, a just and famous system, but it has a biblical distaste for usury. And that's why they decided to employ these little electronic brains.

What they do now is this: a corps of girls, human enough, take your tax return and with a few well-chosen taps on a keyboard reduce its hieroglyphics to a pattern of perforations on a regular business machine card. The card looks roughly like a pocket calendar that has been punched over and over by a very neat and conscientious train-conductor. The girls then feed these cards into the machine at the rate of eight hundred a minute. The machine tubes warm up. A switch is thrown. The tubes or valves flicker and there is a scurry of little lights across the machine panel, about as swift as a falling star. Your tax return is checked, errors discovered and corrected, necessary refund or extra payment noted, and the amended form comes out with the offending mistakes circled in red and the correct total printed. It would take a well-adjusted taxpayer, with a flair for differential calculus, about three days to do this calculation. Just to turn the knife in the taxpayer's wound, the machine does it all in a seventieth of a second.

If this is what baby can do, what is the function of the parent monster who was reared at Harvard? I went up to Madison Avenue the other afternoon to find out, to take a look at Poppa, whose full legal name is the Selective Sequence Electronic Calculator. It does not look like Boris Karloff in a coat of mail. It does not even look like a power-house, or a big radio set. It looks like a big and beautiful room. Which is all the more menacing because to begin with, you have nothing to fight. There is a room, about as big as a hotel lobby. There are marble floors. The walls are nothing but three banks of vacuum tubes enclosed in sliding glass panels and framed in stainless steel. In the middle of the floor is a big unit that looks like a streamlined organ console. It is in fact called the console and is also in stainless steel. Here sit two girls over hundreds of switches. They throw a dozen of them and look over to one of the walls. Across the wall there is a flurry of lights. And one of the girls says, 'Yeah, I guess it's all right.' There are two other units on the floor, in stainless steel and glass. One introduces – on those same little business cards with holes in – the problem that's to be solved by this inaudible and invisible brain. Another unit, much like the first, is a printer that prints up the results in exquisite electronic typing. You'll be relieved to hear, as I was, that there *is* a problem being worked on. The silence is appalling. It is broken from time to time by a momentary chatter or buzz, like a dentist drilling around a cavity. That's the big brain actually at work.

What sort of problem does the brain figure out? Well, this machine naturally isn't interested in anything that would ever disturb an accounting department. For such trifles there is a little offspring called a Calculating Punch, with a mere twelve hundred tubes, which will do in one second flat any big business problem entailing adding, subtracting, multiplying and dividing, with a couple of five-digit numbers that require, say, seventy-nine separate multiplications or sixty-five divisions. Adding and subtracting of course is not so slow.

No, the monster is reserved for the kind of equations that have to be worked out in the physical sciences. It just did a little job of atomic physics for Princeton University. I might be able to explain this more lucidly to you, if the girl who outlined the problem to me had not been a beautiful girl. When you come in off the street to be greeted by this vision, you might think you were meeting a charming floorwalker. But she turned out to be a college graduate who majored in mathematics and then took the course in electronic calculation at a college the business machine company runs for its demonstrators. (The great brain, by the way, cannot tell you her telephone number.) She said that Professor Niels Bohr, the Danish physicist, announced to the scientific world the impressive theory – I'm told it's impressive – that the nucleus of a uranium atom was much like a drop of water and splits unevenly. The only snag in the way of this discovery was the prospect, or the probable certainty, that a drop of water splits evenly. You will simply have to take it on trust that to find out how drops of water behave would engage expert physicists in a calculation taking three generations to compute, or one very healthy mathematician about a hundred years. No point in following that line of thought then. But the Princeton physics department put it up to Poppa. One of the absurd and laughable things about Poppa is that although he can do inhuman subtraction and division – he can even carry four hundred thousand digits in his head stored up on hand in what's called a memory unit – you have to tell him exactly *when* to go into action on each step. He tends to sit around in the lobby like a house detective till the girl at the desk hands him a number. That's what takes the time – punching out those cards to tell him at what stage to add, when to switch to long division, when to square something, when to subtract. Poppa's quite a moron in his own fabulous way. However, they lined up the order of the sequence of problems and fed them into the banks of twinkling lights. And it took Poppa just less than four days – one hundred and three hours. Dr

Bohr, and the Princeton physicists, and the world of physics, knew the answer – surprise, surprise – a drop of water splits unevenly. They can now proceed with Dr Bohr's earth-shaking theory.

Poppa has also recently obliged the Navy by computing the rate of shock wave reactions. He has done a very complicated problem set by an oil company: to figure out the effective rate of pumping to keep the oil pure of salt and mineral saturation. For an observatory he plotted in a day or two something that would have taken years and years – the orbits of five planets between 1780 and 1960. When I was there they had just finished printing up a vast calendar recording the location of the moon at midnight and midday for every day of the past hundred years. Some star-gazer was eager to know this. Don't ask me why. Poppa was presently engaged on a problem slipped to him by the Atomic Energy Commission – a problem that no humans anywhere could even attempt. It was to take the brain five and a half months. Working, by the way, twenty-four hours a day, because if you switch off his power, the brain simply loses track of the four hundred thousand digits he's carrying in his memory unit (for use at various stages of a problem) and falls into a carefree coma indistinguishable from Dr Einstein on a fishing trip. It takes days to warm him up again and get some sense back into him. (Incidentally, if ever the girls feel skittish or mad at him, they can throw the wrong switches, or overload a few tubes, and plug him into an actual nervous breakdown.)

Although Poppa is in great demand for Government problems, he and his brood can be rented by private firms. In the spirit of our times, they are available to the Government free of charge (for a dollar a year, that is) for the solution of military problems. But if you are a peace society who'd like to discover, say, a reliable formula for a quiet life, that – as Chico Marx once said – begins to run into money. I'm afraid in that case you'd have to hire Poppa at the regular rate of three hundred dollars an hour.

A BELL FOR FATHER SERRA

In the spring of 1949 a society of American Christians and Jews heard about an old forgotten bell rotting away in California. They dusted it off and put it aboard a plane with a Franciscan priest. He flew the bell to New York and Paris and London and half of Europe and was in California again in time to get it back for Easter to its resting-place in the hot Santa Lucia mountains, inland from the coast of central California. At dawn on Good Friday it was back where it started from. And they rang it again in the vague, poetic hope that it would recall across the centuries the voice of an old man with bronchitis and a lame foot, who in the same place in the midsummer of 1771 had lifted this bell over an oak-tree and cried aloud to a solitary Indian standing by: 'Come, O Gentiles! Come to the holy Church. Come and receive the faith of Christ.'

The religious society simply wished to express in a dramatic way the desire of the ordinary people of the West for freedom, and for peace, if peace and freedom can still be had together. The Frenchmen and the Londoners who saw this bell must have thought that the Americans had been a little clumsy in their instinct for drama. There are older bells in Europe. But this bell was chosen for a special reason. It was made by the Russians, about sixty years before the old limping man I mentioned hoisted it over the tree and rang it to his Indian. You may wonder what a Spanish priest, born in Majorca and far from home, was doing in California nearly two hundred years ago with a Russian bell. There is quite a story in it, and I hope to tell you a part of it.

The old man's name was Father Junípero Serra, a Franciscan friar, who had gone up from Mexico into what is now California on the express orders of King Charles III of Spain, to convert the very primitive Indians whom earlier Spanish explorers had described with very little relish. Father Serra would never have taken on this commission, and very likely there would have been no California missions for tourists to admire, if King Charles had not been suddenly worried about the Russians. In the 1760s, his minister at St Petersburg reported to Madrid that Catherine the Great, once she had driven the Turks out of Europe, meant to set up a Russian empire in the Pacific and was already lusting after the California coast. King Charles decided to 'contain' this Russian ambition by sending a military expedition north from the farthest western base of the Spanish empire. This is the long Mexican peninsula that falls into the Pacific from what is now the California coastline. Pacifying Alta California, as it is now called, was not a comfortable prospect. The reports that went back to Madrid about the barbarity of the Indians already subdued in Lower California made the planning of the northern march a frightening business. The soldier who had pacified the South had gone mad doing it, until he thought that the only sure way of settling the north and driving out the Indians was to import 'sixty gorillas from Guatemala'.

However, it had to be done. The Russians were already in Alaska, and their ships were reported edging farther south off the coast of Oregon. The Spanish governor at Monterey protested that his garrison was absurdly weak to withstand an attack from Russia or any other great Power that decided to swoop on the lush lands of California.

But when the Russians appeared off the coast of Oregon and down off northern California, they were not smelling out the confines of an empire or craving any land. They were looking for something much more specific. They were looking for the sea-otter. The sea-otter, as you may know, is a placid and funny beast that swims without visible means of support on its back. It is about four or five feet long, is fat and brown, has the whiskers of Colonel Blimp, the round brown face of a well-fed cat. It lies back in the water, its belly protruding, its benign head up and its paws calmly folded across its plump chest. It has a thicker coat than a seal and the ends of its hairs are touched with white, giving it the appearance of a domestic animal that stayed out too long ski-ing and is now

173

resting comfortably in a hot bath. If it were an English beast there would be lots of limericks about it.

Well, aside from its peculiar charm, it had another appeal which the Russians were on to early. Its pelt brought a fantastic price in the China trade. Fishermen from the Aleutian islands had caught some, and when the Russians took them west across the Pacific they found that no pelt ever known to merchant seamen had been thought so precious. The faithful Aleuts, who were the Russians' most skilled otter-fishermen (they had the ability to kneel silently in a boat, as you must for hours, with a spear poised), nosed south and reported sensational schools of sea-otters off the central California coast. To the alarm of the Monterey garrison, the Russian ships would close in, hover a while, and be gone the next day. To the jittery Spanish governor it looked like reconnaissance. It was simply that the Russians had taken another hefty haul and were on their way across the ocean.

The Spanish had a perfectly legitimate reason for resenting another nation coming in on the otter trade. The governors in California had complained for decades to Madrid that they were hampered in developing the province by the absence of quicksilver. In China they had lots of quicksilver, which they prized rather less than the exotic sea-otter pelts. It comes, I think, as a shock to an Englishman to discover that the Spaniards, who had supposedly been blown out of the sea in 1588, were the ranking power throughout most of the New World two centuries later. They had long ago opened up trade routes across the whole Pacific. And they were just beginning to see how their California empire might be stabilized through the exchange value of the sea-otter, when the Russians came. The Russians hired ships on the other side of the continent, in Boston. Soon the Yankees knew about sea-otters too. And the British, as usual, were not far behind. Indeed, the presence of the British within the next twenty years in the waters off what is now Vancouver Island was a far more dreadful omen to the Spanish than anything the Russians did. For it stimulated a row that challenged the Spanish to depend on their historic ally France, just at a time when France could be no help. A French navigator, off on a voyage around the world

for the French Government, wrote a harmless survey of the
ports of the West Coast. He was very well received at Monterey, and coloured his report home with the now epidemic
rumour that the Russians were 'advancing' from the North-
west. King Charles promptly dispatched two commanders to
investigate. They said that both the Russians and the British
were poaching in Spanish waters and meant to establish permanent armed trading-posts all the way down to California.
There is no documentary proof of this intention, but the
investigators went as far north as Nootka Sound, under
instructions to build a Spanish garrison there. By a piece of
ill-luck they found there one American and three English
ships in the Sound. The Spanish commander captured them
and confiscated their cargoes. 'This,' roared the younger Pitt
in the famous words of Groucho Marx, 'means war.' He
mobilized the fleet, ironically called it 'the Spanish Armada'
and challenged the Spanish to fight. They turned inevitably
to France, who unfortunately was busy having her Revolution.
Unable to call the British bluff, Spain gave in, abandoned her
historic policy and with it the last hope of securing her empire
on the Pacific Coast.

It was this Russian panic that produced in an incidental
way the lovely Spanish missions which are now the main archi-
tectural attractions of a trip to California. The King of Spain
happened to be misinformed. The Russians wanted merely a
legal share of the otter trade. And I hope I will not be thought
a fellow-traveller if I mention the historical fact that of all
the enterprising interlopers, the Russians were the most conscientiously legal. The British and the Yankees, on the contrary, made strict promises not to come within so many miles
of the coastline and then resorted to tricks and evasions. They
would lie becalmed off-shore and beg to put into some California cove on the heart-rending pretext that they were short
of food or down with scurvy or had sprung a leak. The
Spaniards took pity on them and let them land. They would
take months for repairs and put on some fine performances
of malnutrition. They would send crews of fishermen out at
night. Suddenly the whole fleet would retire with five hundred
otter pelts.

To cut the otter story short, I should say that when the California otter-fields had been pretty well fished out, the Russians retired and were never thought of as a threat again until 'the Red menace' of the nineteen-twenties had the Pacific Coast by the ears, a threat all the more suspicious because it entailed no Russians you could touch or see. In spite, then, of the foresight of the excellent King Charles III, the Spaniards lost California; and the parts of the Spanish legacy that we remember at all are the lovely place-names of California and the twenty-one missions that Father Serra started.

Which brings us back to him and his bell. On all the Spanish military expeditions in the New World, the accompanying priests were indispensable. They it was who gave to the job of 'pacifying' the native whatever humanity and usefulness it had. They converted the Indians and taught them the rudiments of farming and building. They also kept the diaries of the journeys. The settling of Lower California had been done with great skill and sacrifice by the Jesuits. But in the 1760s the Jesuits were reviled and persecuted everywhere in Europe. France and Portugal expelled them. There were absolutely no grounds, of politics or common decency, for recalling them from the Spanish colonies. But as often happened before and since, history was having one of its obscene and incurable brainstorms. The pressure on Charles III to follow the fashion was intense. And, as always, men of ill-will could find enough plausible reasons to punish the fashionable villain. The Jesuits were a rich company. They did, after all, take a loyalty oath to their order which could easily be taken to imply a dangerous defiance of their allegiance to the King. A rash of rumours broke out in Lower California that the Jesuits had monopolized the fabulous loot of the pearl trade. So Charles III was true to his time and expelled them from the Spanish empire. Their burdens fell on the Franciscans, whose sacred oath was the very dependable one of poverty. It was for this bitter reason that Father Junípero Serra was sent out to Mexico in 1768 and a year later started off with Captain Portolá on one of two land expeditions into Alta California. There were three expeditions by sea, one of which was lost with all hands. The other two crept into San Diego weeks late, a third of their crews alive, the rest dead from scurvy. However, in May of 1769 the four expeditions met in San Diego, where Father Serra said a mass and founded the first of the California missions, San Diego de Alcala.

Whatever were the ambitions of Captain Portolá and his men, the motives of Father Serra were beyond cavil. This man came into a beautiful, but vast, frightening and untilled landscape. He gave himself to the barbaric Indians. He started with an infected foot and ignored Portolá's order to go back. Starting at San Diego, he walked or limped five hundred miles north to the Monterey bay and founded another mission there. He back-tracked a hundred miles over the coast mountains to the spot where in 1949 they rang his bell. He named each mission after the saint whose day coincided with his arrival in the chosen place. The qualifications for such a choice were very tough in the California of those days: the prospect of grass for pasture, good vineyards, and – the eternal California anxiety – water. The company that went along with him and Portolá have left behind them only the memorial of the place-names. They saw an ash-tree, called in Spanish 'fresno', and called the place Fresno. They were taken with the live-oak – the 'encinas' – which abounds over the California hills and named a place Encinas. They were going through Hollywood on the 2nd of August, the Day of Our Lady of the Angels of Portiuncula, which is the name of the chapel in Assisi that cradled the Franciscan order. So the place came to be known – and in spite of some elegant re-christenings later, the City of the Angels, for instance – is still known as Los Angeles. You can get a vivid idea from some of their namings how strenuous this pilgrimage was, how consequential the smallest accident, how welcome an eatable bird. They lost a blunderbuss ('trabuco') in a canyon and named it Trabuco. Fleas bothered them everywhere, and they left the memory in the name Pulgas in four counties. Turning inland one day at the coast, and hungry (they don't seem to have been very good at foraging), they saw a seagull come close and wheel over them. One of Portolá's soldiers sighted it and shot it. They ate it and called the place Gaviota – a seagull.

Altogether, Father Serra walked between four and five thousand miles on his excruciating foot, over scrub desert and through dense mountains and hot valleys without a trail, always putting up a bell and beginning with his cry, 'Come, come and receive the faith of Christ.' The route of his walk is today the route of U.S. 101, a federal highway, and you need hardly ever leave the cement to see the nine missions he founded and the thirteen of his successor. In his seventieth year, Father Serra's health cracked. With that extraordinary endurance given to people who have chosen poverty rather than had it thrust upon them, he walked a final thousand miles around all his missions, saying good-bye to the Indians and the helpers left behind. On his way to San Francisco, at Carmel, he died.

He is the first and noblest of a great, and not much prized, American tradition; the priests who crossed the seas and tramped the enormous curve of wilderness from San Diego, California to St Xavier, Montana in order to care for a few Indians or trappers. Junípero Serra, De Smet, Ravalli, Megarini, Prando and Father Point. They accepted the terrible emptiness of the West as the good ground to work in, to tame it if possible, and where it could not be tamed they admitted defeat with grace. In an age when – perhaps inevitably, I don't know – we give in to bureaucracy in politics, in education and in religion, it may be no more than sentimentality that makes us admire again these men who lived out their Catholicism in the fearful innocence of its Founder.

At this moment, in the Vatican, a postulator is at work, and has been for many years, documenting the life of Father Serra to see if there is enough evidence to make him a saint. He would of course have had to perform a miracle. And on the face of the record, the Devil's Advocate appears to have the edge. For though in personal things Father Serra was meek and gentle, he was not all sweetness and light. He had a mania for self-torture which even the faithful would now, I believe, think unhealthy. He burned himself with a candle to stay awake at his prayers. His infected foot was his own doing : he deliberately let insects and mosquitoes eat on it and refused all treatment. Everyone who was with him or has read the record is agreed that he was a totally fearless and single-minded missionary. But in argument he was also 'enthusiastic, battling, keen-witted, almost quarrelsome'.

Even so, a non-Catholic, even a heathen with a decent pride in his country, may hope that somewhere in the Vatican Library they will find that miracle.

SIX TYPICAL AMERICANS

Before I left to go off on a trip around this continent an old friend turned up in New York. He is a metallurgist, from Cambridge (England), and he was making his first visit to the United States. I had not seen him in sixteen or seventeen years. Back in those days my own interest in metals was not exactly raging, but this man had been, in the brisk days of our youth, the treasurer of a college dramatic society I had something to do with. He is still the treasurer. You might think that that is a slender thread by which to hold a friendship. But having become a reporter since I last saw him, I had come to be interested in lots of things that would have bored me stiff twenty years ago. It is one of the rewards of a reporter's life that he is always meeting people who are experts in fascinating things he never knew existed. I have become, down the years, interested in metals, especially light metals. And so at our first reunion in seventeen years we had the odd and refreshing experience of two old friends talking about none of the things that brought us together and talking madly about the only thing that in the interest of friendship was always politely ignored.

Then we parted. He to go off on a round of factories – Buffalo, Toledo, Pittsburgh, looking for the English equivalents of his speciality; I to take a train South and look for no equivalents. It is necessary for reporters to do this everywhere, lest they get too confident about the nation and the people they are reporting. It is essential in the United States where the mere size of the country encourages you for your self-respect to think of the other regions of the country in terms of what we call types: the typical Southerner, the typical Californian, the typical steel worker, New Englander and so on. But it is not a reporter's job to tell you what are the correct generalizations. It is to report what he sees, and if it doesn't fit into generalizations no harm is done. And the great good that you reap from going thousands of miles to discover the typical American is that you don't find him. You simply marvel again, as you do on any other continent, at the variety and richness of God's creatures. For America is not a bigger Britain. It is a bigger Europe.

So what I am going to do is to tell you briefly about six Americans I met on the road. The only thing they have in common is that they are Americans and that they came my way. But they are all typical. And I shall leave it to you to write the moral, if any.

And who were these fascinating creatures? The first I met when I went aboard a train in Richmond, Virginia, for the trip to New Orleans. I looked quickly around the car, or carriage, to pick out somebody who might be fun to talk to. First thing I saw was a clergyman. The seat by his side was empty. So I plumped down. He was, I should think, in his late thirties or early forties. He had a soft, pale face, with steely-blue eyes, and many wrinkles around them. He was a placid, urban type, I figured, and when he spoke, and there was no Southern accent, I knew him for a Midwesterner. I thought to myself, he runs a church in a fashionable suburb of Cleveland or Cincinatti. Well, he came from Pittsburgh. And he was a priest. I might have known that from his collar in reverse, for there are about sixty denominations in the United States that dress like you and me. The chances are that a reverse collar means a priest. This man had been visiting his parents in Pittsburgh for the first time in four years. He was going back 'home', as he said. And where was home? Home was in the extreme south of Arizona, in the middle of the desert and the wilderness. He was a missionary priest on the reservation of the Papago Indians near Ajo. He lived, as they did, in a mud hut braced with cactus ribs and ministered – as priest, doctor, builder, sports coach – to several hundred Indians. There are about seven thousand Indians on this reservation, but it is a big one, running north from the Mexican border for about a hundred miles. He worked in one of the parent villages and was far from any other white man. He nursed them and in many ways helped them make the best of a poor life, sustained mostly by growing beans (Papago means 'the bean people') in a barren land to which hardier tribes – the Apache and then the even hardier whites – had forced them. But the important thing was – he shared this life with them. His pale face came not from a fashionable suburb but from always going covered in the blazing sun. The wrinkles around his eyes also. Before we settled in for the night, he reached in his pocket and took out a little pack. 'Gum?' he said.

The next two were a boy and a girl. A soldier and a girl. We stood in the hot dry night air at one in the morning, waiting for a train at an Arizona station. Nothing but the purple arc of sky and at the end of the platform the silhouette of a cottonwood tree lapped by a hot breeze. The stars big as sunflowers. The yellow cabs dozed in formation like enormous wasps. A coloured porter sat propped against the stanchions of an express truck. His arms were folded and his cap tilted over his eyes. There was no movement anywhere except for the gasping reflection of an unseen neon sign. A Mexican in a blue coat padded by and went off to the end of the world. The long tracks glistening in the moonlight seemed to bisect the earth.

On a bench was a girl sitting upright with the sleeping head of a soldier in her lap. She was not a pretty girl, but as she sat there with her legs out at a wide angle to leave a friendly lap for the head and shoulders, she was a Madonna, beautifully self-contained – wife, mother, mistress, guardian angel. She smoked a cigarette. And all around her was such a still and inoffensive world that the glowing ash of her cigarette was the only human aggression. And then the train light bristled on the horizon and it came snorting across the desert and in about five minutes it was in the station. The porter came to life again. The soldier woke up with a start, looked up and wildly at the girl for a moment, assembled his sprawling limbs, fixed his cap on his head and got up. He picked up a little bag. He touched his cap. 'Pardon me, and thank you, ma'am,' he said. The girl dusted the ash off her skirt with the back of her hand and without rising said, with a small smile,

'You're welcome, soldier.' He boarded the train and she sat back to wait for her friend or mother, or whoever, due on another train coming the other way.

The fourth American was a big man, sitting opposite me on the way up from San Francisco to Portland, Oregon. He was about six feet five, with a weathered face and fingers fat as baseball bats. He was gloomy about something. He turned out to be a lumber-man, a big lumber-man, from Portland. He'd been talking to shipbuilders in San Francisco. They needed more and more wood for cargo-ships. His problem was that the great forests of the Cascade Mountains – the last remaining stand of forest primeval in America – were beginning to give out. They couldn't replant enough to replace what they cut down. The shipbuilders had said they were very short of wood for dunnage – for the protective covering they use for cargoes or the inner binding of ships' bottoms. Usually they use very cheap wood. They hadn't enough. They dared to suggest the great and beautiful monarch of the north-west forests – the Douglas fir that rises like thousands of cathedral spires on mountain sides carpeted with pines. The lumber-man, a business-man out for a dollar after all, and no sentimentalist about chopping down trees – this man leaned over and tapped the fat tips of his fingers and shook his head and groaned. 'Douglas fir,' he kept saying, 'Douglas fir for dunnage. No, sir.'

The fifth man was a Chicago meat-packer. A prosperous Chicago meat-packer. I'm sure you know the type, everybody does. Well, this man was typical, in his queer way, of many a prosperous Midwestern businessman. His grandfather had been an Irish immigrant who came to work on the railroads. His father had slaughtered cattle and later came to see that what ambles into Chicago as a 'moo' can, with the proper care, go out as steak or a tennis racket. This observation has been the basis of several Midwestern fortunes, and he passed it on to his son, who prudently let other people handle the gut and himself was content to pack the steaks. He was now about sixty, and very wealthy.

One day at the age of about forty-five, when he had had a heavy competitive morning, he sat back at his desk and told himself, 'I simply have to take an afternoon off.' He took it there and then. He went out and by chance into the Art Institute in Chicago, which by expert consent houses the finest collection anywhere of French impressionist painting. The meat-packer was in there for four hours and came out in a terrified glow. He had discovered to his rising astonishment that he liked pictures. Liking is the wrong word. The man made the guilty discovery that he was an unwitting slave of good painting waiting only to be needled into a hopeless addiction. He was not a man who lay around contemplating his passions. He was a man with several telephones. He picked one up – he later, by the way, had a special line put in to take care of his hobby – and called the University. 'Who've you got there,' he asked, 'who can teach me about art?' What sort of art? they asked, fine art, archaeology, Oriental art, frescoes ... ? 'Fine art, rough art – any art,' he said.

He started with a university lecturer in modern painting. He soon employed almost a small faculty of his own. He travelled to every museum and private collection in the United States. He did the same in Europe. He talked to artists, to portrait-painters, and curators, and buyers. He went into paint-manufacturing works. He talked to brush-makers and framemakers. He saw the country and studied the light throughout the day over the landscapes his favourite men had painted. He read all their memoirs and notes. Today in his Chicago home he has the most exquisitely chosen collection – that has everything to do with his taste rather than his learning – of the minor works of a generation of great Frenchmen. One of the greatest of modern art critics has said that nobody alive has a finer flair for assessing the quality of disputed French moderns than this same hale, sixty-year-old, and still unretired Chicago meat-packer.

The last American of my half-dozen and I put him last because it would be impossible to talk about anybody else after him – was a tattooist in San Diego, California. A sleek, foxy-looking little man in his early fifties with a bow tie, an

Adolphe Menjou moustache, and his shirt-sleeves rolled high, his arms blue with writhing snakes, cooch dancers, patterns of lacework, and assorted nicknames. The moment I asked him to open up about his work, he adopted the manner of the government people in charge of defence in the last war. Deliberate, but not so that you could get a word in. Defiant, lest you dared to think that anyone in America was in a better position to feel the people's pulse. He announced, choosing his words with great weight, that 'no trade or business in these United States is a better barometer, you might say' of the American mood and economy. In the first war, he said, 'sailors used to come in here and ask for hearts, and their girls' names. No more,' he said. 'It's a very different picture. Now they seem to want their mothers, just the word Mother.' He sighed. Tattooing, it seemed, wasn't what it used to be in the good old days of private enterprise. 'I mean from the medical angle. I never had a customer yet get blood-poisoning. But in the last twenty years the doctors start hornin' in and settin' up what they call standards. Tattooing today's what you might call a scientific, surgical operation. Sterile needles and all that stuff. That sorta thing makes you pretty leery. They don't encourage tattooing on some parts of the body no more. I have to take it easy. Girls used to come in here, they didn't give a damn what you tattooed on 'em or where. They just want it to hurt, get it? Most guys who get tattooed do it on a dare, just to show they're tough. Sure it hurts. That's the psychology of it. If it didn't hurt, I'd a been outa business thirty-five years ago. But don't forget there are ethics in this game. I don't want to harm nobody. I charge five dollars a square inch for the forearm, ten dollars on the upper arm. I wouldn't touch a chest for fifty bucks.'

I asked him what was the weirdest assignment he'd ever had. He looked me over and shut the door and lit a cigarette. He had obviously told this many times before, but he had to set the stage.

'Well, a woman about two years ago was sick some place up north, Los Angeles – Glendale, I guess. But I mean sick. Had some sort of stomach trouble. And seems the doctor wanted to operate. Well, this guy – a brother – phones here around one in the morning. Wanted to know how much I'd charge to get the way out to Glendale and tattoo her stomach. Now, I mean, I told him that was a tough thing to figure. You see, somebody asks a price on a job and you gotta know where it's gonna be. When I was young at this game I used to quote 'em so much a square inch, thinkin' it'd be a forearm or lower leg or some place where the skin's thin and tight. Hell, if you fix the price, then you have to go to work on a flabby leg. By the time you stretched it so's you can keep the needle goin' smooth, you'd cover an acre. So I figured she was a middle-aged dame and anyway I didn't wanna drive a hundred some odd miles out there. So I says a hundred and twenty bucks. Okay, says the guy, and charge the cab. Honest.

'So I collect the dyes and needles and stuff and I'm on my way. I get out there – to this house, I mean – and go up to the bedroom. It was like a morgue in there. Dark and everythin' and this dame lyin' across the bed screamin' about bein' cut up. Seems she was goin' in the hospital the next day for you know what they call it – observation? She was scared they'd operate on her, and me not get here. Well, I took one look at her and, brother, I gypped myself on the deal. She was enormous. It took me three hours. She'd a been a whole lot more comfortable havin' the operation. I sure was glad to get outa that place. How's that? – what did I write? I wrote what she told me, sort of a note to the surgeon. Clear across her middle: "Do not violate this Body".'

NO SYMPATHY FOR APATHY

Not long ago the gentle E. M. Forster spoke before the American Academy of Arts and Letters. To an audience of distinguished poets, painters, historians and novelists he set up an ideal for the conquering American, whose expression is a little bloodshot these days from being told so often he has come to his first high peak of world power. It was this: 'Man's best chance for harmony lies in apathy, uninventiveness and inertia ... Universal exhaustion would certainly be a new experience. The human race has never undergone it, and it is still too perky to admit that it might result in a sprouting of new growth through decay.'

Mr Forster said this with a weary face and that air of a meditative child whispering in the wilderness which makes him sound sometimes like Gandhi and sometimes like Christopher Robin. Americans may well be depressed by this advice, for they are temperamentally the last people likely to take it. And it was offered to them at a tantalizing time, in the first flush of summer. Only those who have endured a summer on the Atlantic seaboard can know how at that season 'Man's best chance for harmony' does seem to lie in getting down enough beer, expiring enough sweat and keeping at bay, as a distant rustle in the kitchen, the nightly invasions of the cockroach. This coast has theoretically a northern climate, but New York is at the latitude of Madrid. And the summer comes in with a crash of thunder, and thereafter the heat broods over the city till it has turned rancid.

The city's deep streets are hot as the funnels of a stove, the bedrooms like bakeries. From cabs parked on street corners the high voices of baseball commentators rattle out from portable radios, and all there is of the driver slumped inside is one fat, shirtless arm over the door. The Elevated bangs past tenements with all their windows open, dank laundry over the ledges, and vast women shuffling around inside carrying frying-

187

pans or little flower-pots. You see old men sitting on the stoops, and babies spilling over the sidewalks, and cars hooting at little boys darting into the roadway waving baseball bats. You get into a bus and somebody goes down hard on your toe – my toe, that is. And I look up and see through a radiating haze a large pink woman shouting, 'Will you keep your feet to yourself? Somebody's going to be killed one of these days.' And as the bus grinds into gear, and the sudden whiff of carbon monoxide comes up, I hear the voice of a thin man opposite mutter unsmilingly, 'It's a cinch it won't be you, lady.' For three months we shall pad around through sweating streets and blinding light, over grass burned from yellow to brown, and down into the stew of the subway.

But even when the summer exhausts people, and they fall over, the attitudes of their fatigue are nothing short of violent. I walked through Central Park the other day – not a good day, there was high humidity and the sun burned like a copper vat. Nobody could say that the people I saw in the park were full of perkiness or inventiveness. But even in exhaustion, it is rare to see an American who looks cowed or meek. The immense bulk of cheerful derelicts snoozed under trees. Two sailors were spreadeagled in possession of a whole bench to themselves. And though their brows were glistening with sweat, their eyes roved after the girls as sassily as ever. A Negro, fast asleep, sprawled on and over and under a bench, in a position of helpless independence.

These, after all, were the people with a day off, or bums out of a job, or men just arrived in a new port. Everybody else was at work. And when I went down into the subway, the concentration of human sweat and aliveness was immense. I had been going down, day after day in line of duty, to the hearings of a now celebrated perjury trial, and this entailed taking a subway train six miles from my office.

The train I took was an express and does it in seven dreadful minutes. It starts at 42nd Street, makes only one intermediate stop at 14th Street and next comes to rest, panting and dripping oil, under Foley Square, where the law courts are. At 42nd Street the platform was choked with every sort of American face, and body, and shirt, and human shape, and colour of eye and hair, and swarthy males and pretty girls and not so pretty girls, with the trim, bright clothes, the vivid line of scarlet mouth, the flaring nostrils – the animal stare that is the surest sign of the unconscious, un-contemplative American appetite for life, and an acceptance of it no matter how restless, loud, hot or atomic it may be. The train came shrieking round the curve, stopped with a shudder and flung its doors open. A writhing mass of humans fell out, and another mass of humans fell in. One puffing fat man, carrying his coat, his shirt transparent as fly-paper, fell almost on to a very dark, charming-looking girl in front of me. In a flash, her face went into a spasm of anger. She shot black eyes at the big oaf and said in an intense, contemptuous snarl, 'Take it easy! Don't be so – *cute*!' Then we all shoved in, the doors crashed, and her face was calm and charming again as the train swayed and screamed at a perilous pace downtown.

Only an hour later this incident touched off a pathetic irony. In court the defendant's accuser was being questioned about what had been undoubtedly a fairly troubled life. The defence counsel asked him if his brother had committed suicide at the age of twenty-two. He said yes, he had. The counsel read a sentence from the young man, who had tried to persuade his brother to join him in a suicide pact. The sad young man, who in the end went it alone, had written: 'We are gentle people, incapable of coping with the world.' I thought of the brunette with the black eyes, who snarled at the clumsy fat man and then composed her face again without shame or afterthought. She, evidently, could cope. And though a snarl is not an expression taught in the nicest girls' schools, it is an instinctive thing, and on her it looked healthy.

Perhaps New York and other American cities are no place for sensitive souls. And certainly to people who come from places where there is a gentler tradition of public manners and behaviour, New York is raw and terrifying – but, they also always seem bound to add, intensely alive. The question then comes up – how normal, how healthy is spontaneous and intense feeling? The Americans prize it, not only in their theatre and their literature, but in their young. They would no doubt like their children to be delicate and courteous, but if they have to choose they will take them – with a proud sigh – brassy and wild. Even their psychiatrists imply the better chance for happiness of the 'outgoing' child rather than (with an ominous note) the 'withdrawn' child. So shyness is not only at a discount. It is one of the warning signs of emotional trouble that the child-doctors and the child-clinics drop hints to the parent about.

This, I believe, is one of the great differences between the culture of America and the culture of Europe. In Tennessee Williams's poignant play, *A Streetcar Named Desire*, the only scene is a basement flat in a poor section of New Orleans in the thunderous midsummer. Four men – factory workers, ex-G.I.s, a garage mechanic – are playing poker. The hero is a Polish-American, thick-spoken, laconic, with a magnificent body. His wife is a cheerful girl, leaving the poker-players to their game and gossiping – through one of those bead curtains – with her sister, a gentle, neurotic, fanciful girl school-teacher. Suddenly there is a quarrel and the poker game is up in the air. And so too are the table and the beer bottles. The air is thick with flying wedges of bodies and loud cursing. The husband throws everybody out. He is drunk, anyway, but he too is sensitive in his lumbering way and he can't stand the giggles of the girls in the next room. He smashes the radio the gentle girl keeps turning on. It is a terrible scene. The next morning the place is a shambles. The two sisters come into the dishevelled room. The wife stretches luxuriously, looks at the wreckage and the splintered bottles and laughs. The visiting sister is furious and begs her to leave her husband. She launches into a frantic appeal for what she takes to be the best values of a civilized life between men and women. The wife listens ruefully. Maybe she's right. Then the husband ambles in. And the wife takes a flying leap across the stage and is high in his arms.

This is a universal situation. But in the sounds that the audience make, the way they take it, the feeling comes across on our side of the footlights that the sister is in a bad way, that everything that is lusty and normal is on the wife's side. 'That sister,' said a man walking out in the interval, 'is crazy as a coot.'

In this culture, then, what chance is there for warming to 'inertia, apathy, uninventiveness', which have quite seriously been the mainstay of some Oriental peoples?

I go home and open the paper, and rustle through the ads in a magazine. A man has invented a gadget which can make a blind man fly a plane with safety. All the women's ads are for ways and means to be 'alluring, vital, the life of the party'. The workmen are already laying steam-pipes under the motor parkways, so that next winter the snows will melt as they fall and leave a naked, safe highway in the middle of the blanketed countryside. The campaigns get more active every day in the big cities for subscription funds to keep cancer research going at its current unprecedented pace. The farmers of Kansas own more private planes than those of any other State. Bomb or no bomb, Manhattan is loud with the demolition of whole blocks of little buildings and the drilling of foundations for twenty, and thirty, and forty-storey skyscrapers that are shooting up all over town. In Albany the State historical museum has given a black eye to despairing educators and anxious parents by putting on an elaborate exhibition: 'Two thousand years of the comic strip', from ancient pictographs to the comic supplements of today's newspapers.

And on the political scene, countless men in Washington are angry or panicky enough to start investigations into everything from the care of the atomic bomb to the shortcomings of history teachers in the public schools. What comes out of these investigations is a lot of energy thrown into violent accusation, Congressmen listening and challenging eight hours a day, steno-typists working like wood-ticks, and the restless citizen getting the satisfaction not, perhaps, of the truth, but of knowing that somebody is on his toes and watching out for him.

An American newspaperman just back from Europe told me the other day he'd been struck by the more leisurely and meditative tone of the best European political reporting. 'You people,' he said, 'must be trained in a library. But with us, whether we're writing about an oil deal, or China, or the economic reports of the United Nations, we are always looking for a guy with a gun.'

191

He shook his head. But that was pure politeness. There was an unregenerate gleam in his eye. He went off – to look for the guy with a gun, leaving the solid implication that America may end in spontaneous combustion, but never in 'apathy, inertia, uninventiveness'.

IT'S A DEMOCRACY, ISN'T IT?

I was standing on the corner of Lexington Avenue on a Sunday in May waiting for a bus. It was a gorgeous day, hot and golden, and there were not many people around. Sunday is more than a bearable day in New York because for one thing there are about a million less cars than usual. No trucks. Suburbanites in for the day pointing up and down and walking with their feet out. A couple of cabs parked outside a lunch-room, the drivers gone for a beer. A family or two hand in hand, taking the children off to the park. A well-dressed upper-crust couple coming across from Park Avenue also hand in hand – a very common sight in New York, for Americans are not much concerned in such matters with what looks proper or what the neighbours will think. A good day – the sort of day when, for all the panicky newspaper headlines, your faith in people, and their needs and inclinations, is restored.

Suddenly, I heard a ghost. It was a familiar ghost, an invisible man somewhere in mid-air saying in a brisk monotone – 'Strike. The count is two and two. Runners on first and third.' This lingo, or the language of which this is a snatch, is something you would hear in a hundred places – homes, cafés, saloons, cars – from then till the end of the first week in October. It is a radio sports announcer covering a ball game – a ball game being, as you probably know, a baseball game.

The voice was coming from nowhere. A young Negro couple, arm in arm, was ambling towards me. But the man's free arm carried a little box. Of course, it was a portable radio. They went down the subway steps, and as they pattered down into the darkness the voice went on floating up, more excited now: 'A base hit to left field. Fuselli's in, Rodgers coming into third.' Nobody else on the street seemed to notice or to care. But if you had cared, and wanted for one day to get away from radio, I don't know where you could have gone. Out at Coney Island, thousands of bodies would be lying in close proximity not only to thousands of other bodies but to hundreds of other little boxes, tuned high. And the air would be so full of 'He's out' and 'The bases are loaded' and 'Full count', that you'd have had quite a time knowing what the wild waves were saying.

This little picture is meant to produce a shudder in you. If it doesn't, then Britons are not what they used to be, and their passion for privacy, and what's more for respecting the next man's privacy, is dead and gone. Don't misunderstand me. I approve myself very strongly of this feeling. I share it. But it makes me all the less of an American. Only a week ago, I heard a plonking sound, allied to music, quite faint, coming up through the living-room floor. It was a neighbour in our apartment house who is either six years of age and a promising pianist or forty years of age and a dope ... because she – why do I say 'she', I wonder? – has been stuck on that same piece for a month or two now. I grumbled about the sameness of her repertory, and my twelve-year-old daughter, idling over a book, said, 'Relax, Pop, you don't have to hear it if you don't want to.'

By this simple remark my daughter didn't mean that I could get up and go downstairs and start a riot, or that I could call the police or take out an injunction. She simply meant I should shut my mind to the sound. I made sure this is what she meant, because when I played aloud with the idea of strangling our tinkling neighbour, she said, 'I don't think that's very nice. She paid *her* rent too, you know.'

Now, I should like to say that I am proud of my daughter and usually turn to her for a response that is commonsensical and unshocked (by, so far as I can make out, anything in life). But I wasn't aware she had acquired so young a fundamental mood or attitude of what Americans call democracy. In Britain, one of the minor duties of good citizenship is not to disturb the private life of other citizens. In this country, it's the other way around – not to disturb other citizens who are enjoying their private life in public. That, as you see, is a heavily loaded interpretation of an attitude that is universal among Americans. And there are limits. Just the same, the decision of a Washington court of appeal not to let advertisers broadcast in public buses only shows how far you can go in America without being stopped.

Americans regard most of us born in Britain as dull, decent, amiable people but given to being rather testy about our rights. So 'Relax, Pop,' says my daughter and goes back to reading her book with one third of her mind, listening to the pianist downstairs with another lobe, and at the same time dreaming on all cylinders about some absent male of the species. Quite aside from the principle involved, this attitude entails a considerable physical feat. It is the ability not to hear what you don't want to hear, what the most famous radio critic in America calls 'selective deafness'. He says it is a faculty essential to an enjoyment of American radio, and it is a faculty that most visiting Britons would rather not develop. Because they soon learn, as Mr Crosby – John, not Bing – remarks, that the advertising people are aware of this conditioned reflex and so from year to year, like drug addicts, they increase the dose of the sales talk they cut into the programmes. Still, nobody hearing his favourite comedian or forum discussion or symphony concert bothers to turn off the 'plug'. He lets it chatter on about some soap that 'atomizes dirt' or a toothpaste that is 'kind to gums but murder on film'. And then, the ecstatic announcer stops, and so back to Bob Hope or 'Whither Europe?' or the second symphony of Beethoven.

To watch an American on a beach, or crowding into a subway, or buying a theatre ticket, or sitting at home with his radio on, tells you something about one aspect of the American character: the capacity to withstand a great deal of outside interference, so to speak; a willing acceptance of frenzy which, though it's never self-conscious, amounts to a willingness to let other people have and assert their own lively, and even offensive, character. They are a tough race in this. You are expected – far beyond what other peoples would say were the restraints of manners – to assume that one man's opinion is as good as another's. The expert is an American idol, but only in certain understood fields. He is safe from contradiction if his expertness is in a science – in medicine, technology, industrial research, or in making something with his hands (better, if he uses somebody else's hands, because that shows he has mastered a process which can be left to drones): such things as an automobile, a waterproof watch or a non-riding girdle. But when it comes to ideas about life and love and religion and education and architecture and painting and music, indeed all forms of pleasure, there is a national conviction that an expert is a phoney, or 'wants to be different', and that what matters is you should know what you like and – this is a democracy, isn't it? – speak up and say your piece. It may well be born from generations of living close to many races and many prejudices and temperaments and having to strike a liveable compromise that may not be as smooth as some other societies; but at least it is a society, a going concern, which had to be built not out of a theory but out of the urgent practical need to get along at all.

At any rate, if you want to live here in any spiritual comfort you have to allow for a wide variety of temperament in your friends and neighbours and approve a sharp clash of tastes. An insistence on privacy in such a society looks, as it would not look in Britain, like a form of conceit or neurosis, a refusal to admit the status quo by which you all live. So if the issue ever came up in argument, I think most Americans would say that it is merely elementary good manners and good citizenship to look on yourself as only one member of the community, whether that community is a town, a party, or a family.

It may be what makes Americans so easy-going about their children. I don't know if anyone has ever taken a statistical count, and there may be just as many nagging parents here as anywhere else, but my impression is that if you are what they used to call a severe disciplinarian with children, you get known to the neighbours as a crank. There is a sort of cheerful, unstated assumption that children will grow up and be polite soon enough and that there's no sense for the first fifteen years or so in pretending they are anything but inhabitants of the jungle. (There is a certain family pride in seeing your child become king or queen of the jungle.) The children themselves are of course not aware of being particularly bad or violent or ill-mannered. They have no other system to compare themselves with, and like all children don't even know that any other system exists. Remembering this, you can appreciate that if a six- or a ten- or a fifteen-year-old passes you on the street, looks up and says, 'Hi!' he is paying you far more the respect of genuine liking than if he said, 'Good morning, sir' – which would be a very alien, not to say sarcastic, sound in these parts.

The same sort of tolerance explains too, I think, such a seemingly irrelevant thing as the variety of men's clothes in a big city. There is not among Americans anything remotely resembling the uniform of the English city businessman. They dress for themselves, with their own tastes in ties, shirts, shoes; and this gives to an American street a colour, often a garishness, and it makes it pretty impossible for a foreigner to guess at the occupation of the other men around. With women, it is even more difficult. A flock of girls comes into a restaurant and you can't tell the débutante from the shop girl. I remember a Swedish girl on a ski-ing party watching the swirl of people in the snow and saying, 'Which are the nice people? Who are my kind? Give me a sign.' There are signs. But they are small and subtle and would take her years to learn. And if she stayed here long, she would insensibly shed the signs she sought.

I was taking an Englishman the other night up to my apartment, and as we approached the entrance of the apartment house, I saw a man who lives in the building polishing the radiator of his car. I hissed to call my friend's attention to him as we came close. 'Tell me quick,' I said, 'what sort of an American is this – I mean is he a banker, a real-estate agent, a baseball player or what? – look him over.' My friend leered politely at him sideways. He was a middle-aged dark man, with a black moustache and big eyes. He was hatless. He had on a blue sports coat, slacks of a different colour, a button-down collar and a bright tie. He was polishing away and coughing smoke all over the radiator. Then he bent down to start on the wheels. Standing genially over him was the janitor, saying the utterly meaningless sentence, as we came on it: 'No, sir, not for my money ... but some guys are that crazy, I reckon.' When we got inside I looked at my friend.

'Oh, I don't know,' he said, 'I should say an advertising man or perhaps the owner of a chain of drugstores.'

'That,' I said, as we went into the lift, 'is a dethroned Archduke.'

He was dethroned by the bullet that shot his great-uncle and started the First World War.

LETTER TO AN INTENDING
IMMIGRANT

I was going downtown in the subway and was flattened up
against the door reading the morning paper of a man breath-
ing into my ear. If anybody in this train had had room to
ram his elbow into my lungs, chances are I wouldn't have
noticed it. That would have been just an occupational hazard
of travelling in New York during the Christmas shopping
season. But what I became aware of after a mile or so was a
gentle nudge somewhere down there in the direction of my
floating rib. This was such a friendly gesture that I tried
to swivel my eyeballs in the direction it was coming from. I
saw the upturned face of a man who might have been about
five feet three or, then again, might have been a six-footer
simply frozen at that altitude. He grinned and asked me if my
name was Cooke. I said it was and he said his name was Scho-
field and he'd been in school with me in England twenty ...
well, several years ago. Before we lurched to a stop, his stop,
he had time to tell me that he was working in a big department store downtown and had been over here for just about
two years. I asked him if he was here for good. He gave a
little laugh and said he certainly was. 'I just upped and left,'
he said, and the train stopped and he vanished into the
gasping school of New Yorkers peering at us through the
aquarium windows.

This whole episode didn't last longer than thirty seconds,
but it made me glad for him and set me contrasting his
obvious good spirits with the fate and the faces of other
English people I've run into in the past few years who also
'upped and left'. There was, for instance, an English girl
who decided when the war was over that instead of having
her children come back home to her from Canada, she would
join them over here and start a new life in a new land. Her
boy, it turned out, developed one of those boy soprano

voices of remarkable purity. She began to fret – in the little Canadian town she'd settled in – and think back longingly to the church schools in England where this voice might be trained. Of course, she was homesick for more things than an English boys' choir. It was a useful and sensible excuse to give to friends on this side. She is back in London now, very contented in austerity, and her boy is proudly singing his head off.

I think also of a young man in his middle twenties who came here, hit on a good job and quickly acquired the usual admirations: the bright tension of New York, the vigour and irony of its people, the autumn weather, the food, the women, the motor parkways, the theatre. For a time he didn't seem to notice that this was costing him twice or more what these good things would have cost him at home if he'd been able to get them. He didn't need to notice, because he was a bachelor and such things as insurance and social security seemed like an old man's babble. This young and strapping Englishman was undoubtedly by now uprooted. His enthusiasm for many American customs was really a surprised contempt for his own previous ignorance of them. This is not a good basis for permanent admiration and he began to lose some of them, as he came to take them for granted. His job didn't pan out, and he found in the short and ruthless space of one month that New York is a bad town, and America a bad country maybe, to be poor in. With what he had left he went to Jamaica. Restlessness of course is a personal thing, but there was a conflict in it that I've noticed in other Britons who've sailed in here with shining eyes and left after a time in a mixed mood that is not pleasant to admit, for it is a mixture of disappointment and defeat. There is surely nothing to be ashamed of in disappointment. But many of these intending settlers can hardly fail to feel that American life is a far more severe challenge than they had figured on, and it has beaten them.

A century ago the whole adventure was, I think, materially harder on the people who made it, but psychologically not so tough. They knew before they ever left home that they were coming to a land with many less material comforts than

Europe had to offer. They knew that the essential qualifications were physical hardihood, self-reliance, cheerfulness in the face of the adversity that was bound to come sometime, an indifference to social niceties, and a shrugging acceptance of dirt, bad luck, violence and bankruptcy. The visitors who didn't prepare themselves for these hazards had nowhere to turn for sympathy. Their criticisms sounded niggling and effeminate. Thus in 1820, Washington Irving described such Englishmen: 'They miss some of the snug conveniences and petty comforts which belong to an old, highly-finished and over-populous state of society; where the ranks of useful labour are crowded, and many earn a painful and servile subsistence by studying the very caprices of appetite and self-indulgence. These minor comforts, however, are all-important in the estimation of narrow minds.'

It sounds just like a British criticism of the travelling American today. Only the other day a young American film star (who was born on a small farm) caused a commotion in an 'old, highly-finished' hotel in Paris by demanding an air-conditioned room.

Nowadays an Englishman's complaints would not be likely to turn on such things. Now the material scales are weighted in America's favour. Today you can cross the three thousand miles of the American continent and never want for a private bathroom, a cement highway, a night baseball game, an airplane connection, a pair of nylon stockings or a gallon of ice-cream in six different flavours.

But the catch is that America is no more willing than it has ever been to give these things away for free. They are not in this country the luxuries that a secure upper class once exacted from a swarming and servile lower class. They are the minimum demands of comfort made by a population as fertile as its resources, in a country where comfort has accordingly turned into big business. A share of that comfort, a bigger share of satisfying and ingenious comfort than any nation has ever known, can be bought by any worker with a steady wage. But the measure of that steady wage is the energy he can maintain. Visiting teams of British factory managers have remarked on the tenacity with which American

201

workers compete through incentive schemes. You have only to lean out of any midtown window in New York, or in a score of other cities, to notice the furious concentration and energy of construction workers while they are on the job. At five o'clock they will quit like an exploding light bulb, but up to that moment they haul and hammer and drill and bulldoze with fearful zest.

A little time ago I left my office, as I usually do, about seven in the evening (not having the instinctive zest of the natives) and saw that the whole lobby of the skyscraper office-building – which spans something like the floor-space of Piccadilly Circus – was covered with tarpaulin from which arose a network of ladders and scaffolding, a whole series of wooden platforms running about seven or eight feet from the ceiling. This scaffolding alone looked as if it might take a day or two to put up. But none of it was there at five o'clock when the offices of this building disgorged their three or four thousand employees. However, this was only the preparation for the job in hand. The job in hand was the painting of the whole of this great ceiling, which is about thirty feet from the ground. Sixteen men at various intervals were already up on the platforms and beginning to wave a kind of big flat brush, which from my angle looked about as wide as the tail of a whale. I had to come back that night to my office to catch the midnight news. There was not a man in sight, nor a paintbrush, nor any tarpaulin or scaffolding. The night cleaners were already busy with their monster vacuum cleaners. And the ceiling was gleaming with its new paint.

This kind of shock greets the stranger wherever he goes. You have your house painted, or a wall knocked down, or new lighting sockets put in. And I should warn any incurable English perfectionist that half the time you will get a finished job something less than what would satisfy a first-rate craftsman. But this is neither their aim nor their interest. They do what they contract to do with remarkable speed and skill. Then they clean up your disordered home in a final cheerful burst and are on their way back to their wives, their shower-bath, their steak and television sets. These men get paid better than any working-men have ever been paid, allowing for the

202

exchange, the higher cost of living, and all that. The painters I just told you about were earning a hundred and thirty dollars a week – forty-six pounds ten – which will take care of quite a lot of high cost of living. (I ought to add, though, that they pay just about the same, forty-six pounds ten, one week's wages, for the monthly rent of a small house.) If they work this way, they will keep their job. If they don't, they won't: that is the simple, brutal rule of life in America in prosperous times.

You can see how hard it is to start from scratch in this country, which already has a labour force of over sixty millions, and the fiercest kind of competition at all levels, from the labourer to the managing director. It sounds like a nightmare, and it may well be so to gentle, sensitive people who have no sympathy with the fight for life and merely want to earn enough money to give them leisure in their evenings, some fields to walk across, a little light and air. In the big cities of America these things too come at a high price. I sometimes feel that the house agents and real-estate men in all the big cities have measured every building and gauged exactly how many cubic inches of every little room are touched by sunlight for a few hours of the day. That room, once the estate agents discover its secret, will have its rent doubled. Several million middle-class families in the cities of England have a little back garden which they could reproduce in New York for a mere five thousand pounds.

It is hard for the romantic Englishman or woman to talk to Americans about these anxieties. Apart from seeming a chronic complainer, you will also tend to sound to Americans like a kind of immigrant they were long ago warned about. Washington Irving was on to this type too and wrote of them: '... they may have pictured America to themselves an El Dorado, where gold and silver abounded, and the natives were lacking in sagacity; and where they were to become strangely and suddenly rich in some unforeseen, but easy manner'.

Well, that sort of character will be around for quite a time yet, but he grows increasingly peevish. It may be that present-day America, or rather the movie and magazine myths about it, attracts a semi-playboy type that is too soft to take the known risks of a hundred years ago. Unfortunately, the austerity and anxiety of Europe produce, too, many unassuming and honest people who are looking for nothing more than a competence and a little peace and quiet. To the newcomer there is no easy guarantee of it. Sons of wealth can have it without any effort, for this country now has the biggest class of hereditary rich of any nation on earth. But for the newcomer there will be little concern about how he lived or what he was used to, or the kind of people he moved among. If he wants the same society in America, he must buy his way into it. Not what you seem to be, but what you prove you can do: that is still, for the stranger, the persistent pioneer requirement. You have been warned.

MORE ABOUT PENGUINS
AND PELICANS

For further information about books available from Penguins please write to Dept EP, Penguin Books Ltd, Harmondsworth, Middlesex UB7 ODA.

In the U.S.A.: For a complete list of books available from Penguins in the United States write to Dept CS, Penguin Books, 625 Madison Avenue, New York, New York 10022.

In Canada: For a complete list of books available from Penguins in Canada write to Penguin Books Canada Ltd, 2801 John Street, Markham, Ontario L3R 1B4.

In Australia: For a complete list of books available from Penguins in Australia write to the Marketing Department, Penguin Books Australia Ltd, P.O. Box 257, Ringwood, Victoria 3134.

In New Zealand: For a complete list of books available from Penguins in New Zealand write to the Marketing Department, Penguin Books (NZ) Ltd, P.O. Box 4019, Auckland 10.

Look out for these from Penguins!

CHARMED LIVES
Michael Korda

The story of Alexander Korda and the fabulous Korda film dynasty starring Garbo, Dietrich, Churchill and a cast of thousands.

'Charmed lives, doubly charmed book ... Comments, jokes, experiences; and at the heart of it all there is Alexander Korda, powerful, brilliant, extravagant, witty, charming. And fortunate: fortunate in his biographer. Few men have the luck to be written about with so personal an appreciation, so amused, yet so deep an affection' – Dilys Powell in *The Times*

THE WHITE ALBUM
Joan Didion

In this scintillating epitaph to the sixties Joan Didion exposes the realities and mythologies of her native California – observing a panorama of subjects and events, ranging from Manson to bikers to Black Panthers to the Women's Movement to John Paul Getty's museum, the Hoover Dam and Hollywood.

'A richly worked tapestry of experiences' – Rachel Billington

THE SEVENTIES
Christopher Booker

From the rise of Mrs Thatcher to the murder of Lord Mountbatten, from the energy crisis to the trial of Jeremy Thorpe, from the Cult of Nostalgia to the Collapse of the Modern Movement in the Arts ... In this series of penetrating essays Christopher Booker explores the underlying themes which shaped our thoughts and our lives in the 'seventies.

'Booker is quite compulsive' – *Punch*
'Constantly stimulating ... savagely funny' – *Evening Standard*

Alistair Cooke

'One of the most gifted and urbane essayists of the century, a supreme master' – Benny Green in the *Spectator*

The *New Statesman* said of him that 'he is always delightful and at his best a master', the late Harold Nicolson called him 'the best broadcaster on five continents'. Penguin are delighted to publish two further volumes of Alistair Cooke's letters, selected from the longest-running one-man series in broadcasting history, 'Letter from America'.

TALK ABOUT AMERICA
Letters from America 1951–1968

From Vietnam and changing racial attitudes to the new Californian and Alcatraz, as always, Alistair Cooke's comments on American life are distinguished by his pungent language, his clarity and commonsense and by his abiding enthusiasm for current affairs.

THE AMERICANS
Letters from America 1969–1979

With an engaging blend of urbanity and charm, Alistair Cooke talks about Watergate and Christmas in Vermont, gives opinions on jogging and newspaper jargon, creates memorable cameos of Americans from Duke Ellington to Groucho Marx, and discusses a host of other topics – all in that relaxed, anecdotal style which has placed him among our best-loved radio broadcasters.

and

SIX MEN

With these superbly realized portraits, Alistair Cooke brings to life six men he has known and admired during a lifetime of journalistic encounter: Charles Chaplin, Edward VIII, H. L. Mencken, Humphrey Bogart, Adlai Stevenson and Bertrand Russell.
'The journalist's memoir par excellence ... top of the class' – *Newsweek*